ROUTLEDGE LIBRARY EDITIONS:
WORK & SOCIETY

Volume 9

I0110200

WORLD LABOUR
RIGHTS AND
THEIR PROTECTION

WORLD LABOUR RIGHTS AND THEIR PROTECTION

JAMES AVERY JOYCE

R Routledge
Taylor & Francis Group

LONDON AND NEW YORK

First published in 1980 by Croom Helm Ltd.

This edition first published in 2024
by Routledge
4 Park Square, Milton Park, Abingdon, Oxon OX14 4RN

and by Routledge
605 Third Avenue, New York, NY 10158

Routledge is an imprint of the Taylor & Francis Group, an informa business

British Library Cataloguing in Publication Data
A catalogue record for this book is available from the British Library

ISBN: 978-1-032-80236-7 (Set)
ISBN: 978-1-032-81329-5 (Volume 9) (hbk)
ISBN: 978-1-032-81331-8 (Volume 9) (pbk)
ISBN: 978-1-003-49927-5 (Volume 9) (ebk)

DOI: 10.4324/9781003499275

Publisher's Note
The publisher has gone to great lengths to ensure the quality of this reprint but points out that some imperfections in the original copies may be apparent.

Disclaimer
The publisher has made every effort to trace copyright holders and would welcome correspondence from those they have been unable to trace.

World Labour Rights and their Protection

James Avery Joyce

CROOM HELM LONDON

© 1980 James Avery Joyce
Croom Helm Ltd, 2-10 St John's Road, London SW11

British Library Cataloguing in Publication Data

Joyce, James Avery
  World labour rights and their protection.
  1. Employee rights
  I. Title
  331.2'596   HF5549.5.E/

  ISBN 0-85664-889-2

Printed and bound in Great Britain by
Redwood Burn Limited Trowbridge & Esher

CONTENTS

In friendship, for
ARCHIE EVANS
who gave thirty years
of exemplary service
to the ILO

ACKNOWLEDGEMENTS

It is obvious that a book of this kind must be based on a substantial amount of documentary evidence and in-depth research. However, as the author's aim is to attract the widest interest to so vitally important a field of human relationships, every effort has been made to render the text as a smooth running narrative. Hence, footnotes and other source references are reduced to a bare minimum. Where there has been a high condensation of the original data – as, for example, in the brief summaries of case studies in Chapter 6 – the basic documents which have been relied on have been indicated in a single footnote, so that the more specialised reader might check such sources for further information or instruction. The several Appendices seek to expand some of the essential texts for ready reference.

The incomparable documentary resources and archives of both the International Labour Office and the European Office of the United Nations in Geneva have been drawn upon heavily. So have the time, expertise and generosity of many of their specialised personnel, who are, of course, in no way responsible for the author's own views and prejudices, so boldly set forth in the present book. For a more detailed analysis of some of the background issues expounded in these pages the reader is referred to the author's *The New Politics of Human Rights* (Macmillan, 1978), and *Human Rights: International Documents* (Sijthoff, Netherlands, 1978).

James Avery Joyce
June 1979

INTRODUCTION

Although this book focuses its main arguments on what may seem to be, to some readers, a limited segment of the population – the worker in his job – the story that it tells reaches into every phase of civil liberties. Human rights are universal and indivisible. While here we are concerned primarily with the working rights of a professional group, still called the 'working class', we are also exploring the same fundamental freedoms shared by all classes in all parts of the world.

The attack by military usurpers and other elevated crackpots on the rights of the 'workers' is an attack on the dignity and worth of the individual everywhere. For that reason, the special area of our concern encompasses far more than our title would seem to convey at first glance; for we are coming to grips with the threatened moral interests and physical well-being of all mankind.

Our field of enquiry is somewhat narrowed by the fact, however, that we have to focus on a special type of subject matter, namely, the organisation of labour. The broader aspects of human rights and their infringements by sovereign governments are dealt with elsewhere by this author.[1] Dictatorships are no respecters of persons and, in the final analysis, all human rights are political.

Within the special field treated, it must be noted also that non-observance of the high standards set by international instruments as applied to general social conditions may not, of itself, provoke specified complaints from individual workers. In other words, we are not principally occupied with the prevailing political and economic situation in the countries surveyed, but with the legitimacy of individual complaints and how they can best be alleviated.

The techniques developed by the imposed military regimes which have been proliferating during the last decade or so (the period of this study) are a far more serious matter. They are characterised by certain classical devices aimed at breaking the will of the individual dissident or organised political opposition to their tyranny. How does this work? There is the isolation of 'subversive' elements from the mass of the people. Where there exists open war, as in Vietnam or Zimbabwe-Rhodesia or Palestine, the non-compliant members of the population are cooped up in prisons or 'protected' villages and shut off from their homes or work-places.

South Africa has the largest and worst record of attempts to suppress a whole people. But the method depends on the historical origins or geographical circumstances of the take-over. While the crushing of human rights in South Africa is a deliberate act of state policy, the case of Israel is *sui generis*. Its continued military occupation of foreign territory captured in war is itself a violation of human rights, irrespective of the treatment of the indigenous peoples. Under Latin American dictatorships opponents are abducted or just made to 'disappear'. Bishop Candido Padim of Brazil has pointed out the peril of these upstart military castes. He says: 'The function of aristocratic élites of colonial times is now undertaken by the armed forces, who believe that they are endowed with sufficient enlightenment to discern the true path for the nation.'

Imprisonment without trial and exile have been widely practised in Chile and Argentina in the 1970s, where political opponents have the option of spending indefinite periods in jail or of fleeing their country, with all that that means in terms of complete dislocation of family and professional ties. Worse, sophisticated methods of gathering information by torture and psychological intimidation, as well as infiltration by spies and provocateurs into the home or workplace, the tapping of telephones and opening of mail have become instruments of government. The dismissals and other penalties inflicted on certain workers in the Soviet Union and Czechoslovakia for merely setting up independent trade unions or monitoring groups will not be overlooked in these chapters either.

It is because the particular rights affecting the world's 'workers' which we are reviewing in this book take their rise from certain basic principles of international law, that we must begin our study by outlining just what those principles are and where they can be found.

Hence, Part One seeks to answer the primary question: 'What *are* workers' rights?' This general survey begins in Chapter 1 with what the Universal Declaration of 1948 says about them; followed by various Covenants bearing directly on workers' rights. Then, in Chapter 2 we examine what is called 'international labour legislation', within the framework of the ILO Conventions. Chapter 3 explores a more restricted, but no less important, area in the European Convention and its machinery of implementation.

Part Two first outlines in Chapters 4 and 5 *how* the UN and the ILO respectively deal with complaints, and then goes on to itemise, in Chapter

6, specific infringements by selecting certain countries whose notorious treatment of workers and their organisations have become matters of world-wide public scandal. It is a long chapter but, unfortunately, the 'black list' of nine countries we have selected by no means exhausts this legacy of shame. Chapter 6, on specific cases, will form the heart of our enterprise. Yet our choice is wide and varied enough to counter the shallow excuses uttered by the indicted governments and their partisans, who invariably protest: 'Why pick on us? What we do to our trouble-makers we do legally and because our national security demands it!'

The obsession with 'national security', real or imagined or prefabricated, has politicised human rights to such an extent that only a fundamental change in the political order itself can assure them. As this point is so frequently overlooked in current human rights discussions, we should recognise from the start that the suppression of civil liberties in what have been called 'national security states' is not a passing phenomenon. Basically, violations of human rights are integral to the day-to-day policy of these regimes, rather than mere deviations from normal. A national security state is by definition a violator of human rights. It is not the 'laws' that need changing but the state itself. It lies outside the scope of this book, however, to deal with the essential political-cum-military changes that would free the prisoners and set in motion regimes imbued with social justice.

As set out above, states that put the pretext of 'security' before everything else do not fall into a regular pattern. For example, members of an independent church-sponsored labour organisation trying to raise the wages of South Korea's low-paid factory workers have encountered arrests, sporadic violence and heavy government pressure, because the government and factory management are attempting to suppress the movement as part of their campaign to keep wages low and assure the competitiveness of South Korean exports. Then there is the relatively poor state of Israel, which spends a higher proportion of its GNP on armaments than any other nation in the world, and which claims a democratic form of government for its own people, but subjects over two-and-a-half million indigenous population to a form of a second-class citizenship imposed by military control, contrary to the UN Charter and international law.

Yet other states have inflicted a far worse form of military 'occupation' on their own peoples by declaring a state of siege or emergency, or martial law. These regimes, such as that formerly existing in Uganda and in some other African states, concentrate in a few hands the combined use of terror, a rigid censorship and direct control of the mass media, as well as an educational system and a civil service infiltrated by a dominant military caste. Yet, although such upstart regimes sometimes seem to enjoy considerable popular support, they have ultimately failed to manipulate or control the trade unions and peasant movements on any significant scale, even when they have killed or imprisoned their leaders.

So, in Part Three, we take this important question a stage further and, in a brief Chapter 7, indicate how trade unions are reacting to the assault on freedom of association. Plainly, trade union organisations in authoritarian and quasi-fascist states, with their brutal caricatures of 'controlled democracy', are facing strains never experienced in the old-fashioned regimes of Western Europe. The examples vary; alongside the thinly disguised authoritarianism of Brazil, for example, compulsory conscription was recently imposed in Bolivia on all sectors of the population. In the latter case this brought about the reorganisation of the trade union movement, with government-appointed officials; yet, even then, official endeavour was shattered in 1978 by widespread hunger strikes. Further instances have been detailed in Chapter 6.

Part Three, in fact, shifts the argument outside the delinquencies of oppressive governments altogether. Slowly at first, a new force has been making itself felt in the spread of social justice, throughout the ever widening range of United Nations action. This is the power of the non-governmental bodies (Chapter 8), many of which are legally associated with the UN's Economic and Social Council, under Article 71 of the Charter, thus enjoying 'Consultative Status'. So, Amnesty International, as well as the International Commission of Jurists and other non-governmental organisations, have steadfastly come to the rescue of the world's workers. Moreover, they exert 'grass roots' moral pressure on their own governments and on the international community in a way in which official bodies are precluded.

Yet we are still only at the beginning of the search for longer-term remedies. Part Four, therefore, seeks to round off this preliminary enquiry of ours by looking towards more courageous innovations in the UN family of organisations (Chapter 9), backed by national action (Chapter 10), in developing a more extensive use of the various means of public appeal that are now at our disposal through the mass media.

Finally, it should be noted that there are some things that a book of this kind cannot attempt to do: We cannot delve into the origins or rights and wrongs of the underlying political conflicts that have led or contributed to the violations dealt with here in terms of their impact on the rights of the aggrieved *individuals*; and we cannot attempt to 'balance' the rights and wrongs of a given national situation against similar happenings elsewhere, for example, to contrast Soviet Union policy on trade unions with South African apartheid, or to compare a birching of a schoolboy by a teacher in the Isle of Man with the execution of labour leaders in Iraq.

Nor can we assess the value or effectiveness of national trade union organisations, functioning as political bodies, either in socialist states or 'free enterprise' states.

What *can* be attempted in this short space, however, is to bring together some overriding ideas which the thoughtful reader might find worthy of further exploration, such as the following: The intrinsic importance of impartial investigation and third-party judgment, now being carried out within a permanent global context, for the vindication, if not the outright resolution, of human rights problems arising in the sovereign states; the recent emergence of a close working relationship between the major human rights institutions, especially the interlocking nature of the UN Covenants with the ILO Conventions within the UN system; and the fact that this flexible inter-state machinery, as well as the actions of voluntary bodies in support of it, are far more fruitful in the long run in defending the individual's rights than unilateral political pressures or penal sanctions and threats marshalled by one state against another.

So much of this experience is entirely new. The UN Human Rights Committee, for instance, which was set up to deal *inter alia* with individual complaints, started work only in 1977, though the ILO Conventions go back much further. The mounting volume of complaints of injustice being given utterance today through this new order of social concern is indeed proof that the standards which the world community has so recently set up are challenging national governments to behave differently. Not least is the growing realisation that it is no longer permissible for the sovereign state to act as prosecutor, judge, and executor in its own cause.

It does not follow, however, that the state and the international community should necessarily be in conflict on the protection of human rights and freedoms. As Professor John P. Humphrey of McGill University, Canada, has pointed out:

> The relationship inherent in any human right is essentially one between an individual or individuals and the state. Either the individual has a claim against the state to do or to forbear or he looks

to the state for protection against other individuals who violate or threaten to violate his rights as determined by the law. The relationship between the individual and the state is therefore very close, much closer than his relationship with the international community.

It follows that, while the international community has increasing responsibility for the protection of human rights, the primary responsibility for the achievement of this still falls at the national level. Hence, since states do have the first responsibility, they should be expected to rectify any violation of human rights before a case is acted upon by any international body having jurisdiction in the matter. This principle is reflected in the 'exhaustion of local remedies' rule which is to be found in most of the international procedures set up for the international protection of human rights.

In the pages that follow, this subtle but intrinsic relationship between the individual, the state, and the United Nations system of rights protection will be seen as one of the most fascinating aspects of our study. And to the discerning eye, this evolution of a global conscience concerning neighbours' rights is a step towards a responsible world citizenship that has never before been actualised.

Note

1. J. Avery Joyce, *The New Politics of Human Rights* (Macmillan, London, and St. Martin's Press, New York, 1978).

Part One

WHAT ARE WORKERS' RIGHTS?

1 THE INTERNATIONAL BILL OF RIGHTS

What the late Dr C. Wilfred Jenks called 'The Common Law of Mankind' took a vast step forward when the Universal Declaration of Human Rights was proclaimed by the UN General Assembly on 10 December 1948 (since observed as Human Rights Day) without a dissenting vote. Although not legally binding in itself, it has proved to be the starting point of a new legal order in the world. Much of it is now customary law and a major part of the Declaration has become part and parcel of the national constitutions of over 30 new states. More significant, perhaps, it laid the foundations of a wide range of Covenants and other international legal instruments which are binding, when ratified, on national Governments.

The United Nations Charter of 1945 had affirmed the world's people's faith in 'fundamental human rights and in the dignity and worth of the human person'. A global movement sprang so quickly from the Universal Declaration that its impact on contemporary life was barely understood at the time; but, today, it is reaching into the darkest hell-holes of the dictatorships and military regimes in all continents.

The ramifications of this protection go far beyond any routine definition of 'workers' in the layman's eyes. Take the following somewhat unusual example. Mr R.L. Maharaj, a barrister, was committed to imprisonment for seven days on a charge of contempt of court by the High Court of Trinidad and Tobago. His appeal to the Privy Council in London in 1978 was allowed.

His conviction was set aside on the grounds, first, that on a correct analysis of the facts, he had not committed the contempt of which he was charged; and, secondly, that he had been deprived of his liberty *without due process of law*. It was held that the failure of the trial judge to inform him of the specific nature of the contempt of court with which he was charged contravened a constitutional right in respect of which he was entitled to protection under the Constitution of Trinidad and Tobago.

The Appellant therefore claimed redress in the form of monetary compensation for the period that he had spent in prison. His claim was denied by the High Court of Trinidad and Tobago and by the Court of Appeal of that country. He thereupon appealed again to the Judicial

Committee of the Privy Council, which held that he was entitled to damages, and remitted the case to the High Court of Trinidad and Tobago, and the latter awarded him $50,000 damages. This was clearly a case vindicating the inclusion of Human Rights principles in the national Constitution itself. If the doctrine of judicial immunity were to be used by judges to violate the Constitution it could lead to serious abuses in those countries where judges are subject to political or military pressure by the Executive, as we shall review later.

The Universal Declaration was humanity's unanimous response to the Nazi death camps, the fleeing refugees, and tortured prisoners of war of the Second World War. But it was not a once-for-all reaction. It was, in fact, conceived from the start as a global 'Bill of Rights' to be implemented by two legally enforceable Covenants: the Covenant on Economic, Social and Cultural Rights, and the Covenant on Civil and Political Rights. Both of these came into force following 35 ratifications for both in 1976. So the international law of human rights is really quite recent. But we shall deal in the next chapter with those older forms of enforceable labour law already long in operation as applying to the world's workers under the ILO system of Conventions. The two UN Covenants had at last, however, laid down the *legal* foundation for a world order of human rights, from which nobody on earth was excluded.

That the coming into effect of these two major Covenants in 1976 should have received no, or only casual, notice in the world's press or parliaments, is indicative of the atrophy into which public opinion has fallen, except when shocked or scandalised by some blatant violation of human rights. The 1976 event should not be underestimated. Some of its implications will be spelled out in this first chapter, as they have laid the groundwork for the development of international procedures which will give concrete expression to the obligations that national states have so recently undertaken in the name of their peoples. For without institutions functioning continuously in their service, even the most solemn obligations may sink to the level of pious aspirations.

Since the Universal Declaration was the fountain-head of an ever growing outflowing of new rules of world law, we shall look at it in this chapter by reducing it to its simplest terms, and give a summary glance also at the two major Covenants that spring from it, though their implications in terms of specific labour rights are dealt with in later chapters.

What the Declaration Declares

A Preamble of the Declaration sets out the basic ideas, which are expanded later on in the main text. The Preamble states that 'the inherent dignity' of each member of the human family is the basis of the Declaration. The *individual*, not the state or the Government, is 'the foundation of freedom, justice and peace in the world'. It then goes on: 'disregard and contempt for human rights have resulted in barbarous acts which have outraged the conscience of mankind'. Because of this, it is essential 'that human rights should be protected by the rule of law'.

The Preamble goes on to state that the Declaration is based on the UN Charter, by which member States 'have pledged themselves to achieve, in co-operation with the United Nations, the promotion of universal respect for and observance of human rights and fundamental freedoms'. The General Assembly had proclaimed the Declaration as 'a common standard of achievement for all peoples and all nations'. So every individual in the world, and all Governments and groups, are urged to strive, 'by teaching and education', to promote these rights in every way that is open to them. This is what is meant by 'universal'.

But treaties may be broken. They do represent, however, the strongest form of binding obligation on nations and on their governments today. So a treaty or covenant to protect human rights should also be assembled and put before the governments for signature and ratification, and thus bring the full force of international law behind the Declaration.

Discussion on the Commission on Human Rights showed, however, that it would be preferable to prepare two separate Covenants: one on civil and political rights, and the other on economic, social and cultural rights. Preliminary drafts were completed in 1954 and the General Assembly adopted them in 1966. Hence, both Covenants, which were ratified by the required number of states in 1976, as we have seen, are legally binding on states which are parties to them. An examination of the chief articles of the Declaration will cover also the subject-matter of these two Covenants, but our stress in this chapter will necessarily be on labour rights.

For example, Article 1 states quite simply that 'all human beings are born free and equal in dignity and rights'. Because of this, they 'should act towards one another in a spirit of brotherhood'. Thus, for the first time, an international instrument proclaims the principle of human brotherhood.

The second Article carries the premise further. It states, in part, that 'everyone is entitled to all the rights and freedoms set forth in this

Declaration, without distinction of any kind'. Then it lists a number of categories in which people are frequently divided, but because of the principle laid down in Article 1, these categories – race, colour, sex, language, religion and so on – must no longer affect any individual's rights. Man's personal rights on this planet have nothing to do with his family or his ancestors, the colour of his skin, the language he speaks, his wealth or possessions, or his poverty in worldly goods.

Articles 3-11 centre upon the freedom of the individual and form the heart of the Declaration. Article 3 reads in its entirety: 'Everyone has the right to life, liberty and security of person.' A large number of other rights follow this basic right to life. These are set out in Articles 4-11. Naturally, slavery in all its forms (Article 4) can have no part in civilised society. The history of the fight against slavery has been a continuous one with an important landmark in the League of Nations Slavery Convention of 1926. This struggle over human rights soon led to a powerful attack on what is called 'forced labour', a form of servitude imposed upon individuals by governments rather than by individuals. Here, the ILO had a direct part in investigating working conditions in various countries, leading up to the adoption in June 1957 of its further Convention on the Abolition of Forced Labour. Under this Convention, the states who are party to the Convention undertake to suppress any form of compulsory labour, whether it is used as a means of political coercion or education, or as a method of mobilising labour for economic development – a point we shall take further in the next chapter.

Articles 5-11 bear mainly on the limitations on punishment for crime and they all seek to enforce the Rule of Law. 'No one shall be subjected to torture' (Article 5). 'Cruel, inhuman or degrading treatment or punishment' is outlawed. In Article 6: 'Everyone has the right to recognition everywhere as a person before the law.' The accused person must not be arrested 'arbitrarily' (Article 9) and, when he is brought before the court, he must have all the professional help he needs for his defence, and be entitled to a fair and public hearing by an 'independent and impartial' tribunal (Article 10). Article 11 lays down that punishment can only be meted out after a public trial and after the accused has been proved guilty 'according to law'.

Between Articles 12 and 21 the rights of the individual can be seen to be expanding in a series of concentric circles. For example, Article 12, which in effect lays down the rule that every man's home shall be his castle, is strengthened by Article 16, asserting his 'right to marry and to found a family'. As Article 12 points out, the 'protection of the law against such interference or attacks', could hardly be more essential to man's existence in society. His 'privacy' and his 'correspondence' – and that includes his telephone – and even his 'honour and reputation' are to be protected from any intruder. Article 16 states that 'the family is the natural and fundamental group unit of society'. Hence, the family 'is entitled to protection by society and the State', and 'men and women . . . are entitled to equal rights as to marriage'.

Residence comes up again in Article 13. The citizen 'has the right to freedom of movement' not merely within his own state, but also 'to leave any country, including his own' and to return to his own country. The point of Article 13 is that freedom of movement had been *proclaimed* as a universal right, nearly three decades before the famous Helsinki accords of 1975. Article 14 deals with the possibility of a 'right of asylum', for example, the right of every individual (except those accused of non-political crimes) who has fled from his own country because his political opinions may put his life in danger, to be protected in the land to which he has fled. Several United Nations Conventions protecting the rights of refugees and stateless persons have been adopted, and a High Commissioner for Refugees appointed to assist refugees. A Convention on the Status of Refugees entered into force in 1954, and some 70 states have ratified or acceded to it, pledged to give refugees the same treatment as nationals with regard to religion, access to courts, elementary education, social security, and so on. In 1976 a Declaration on Territorial Asylum was adopted by the General Assembly. But unfortunately, a Plenipotentiary Conference, convened in 1977 to draft a Convention on the *Right* of Territorial Asylum, terminated without reaching agreement.

Yet, in spite of this long delay in attempting to secure legal recognition of the rights of a man or woman seeking political asylum, Article 15 insists that 'everyone has the right to a nationality'. As a corollary, the second part of the Article states that no one shall be 'deprived of his nationality', though he may change it if he so desires. Article 17 states that 'everyone has the right to own property' and that no one shall be arbitrarily deprived of his property. While Articles 18 and 19 both take us back to the objective in the Preamble of the UN Charter: 'to practise tolerance, freedom of thought, conscience, and religion', and 'freedom of opinion'. It will thus be observed that the direct phrases of the Declaration go far beyond a prescription for individual freedom. They lay down the essential conditions of how a state should be organised, so that each of its citizens may count for one.

The next two Articles follow up this concept and bring us directly

into the field of labour rights. Article 20 affirms that anyone has the right
to join any association or organisation, yet no one can make him join it
if he does not want to. We shall note in the next chapter that the ILO
adopted in that same year (1948) the Freedom of Association and Protection of the Right to Organise Convention, and, in 1949, the Right to
Organise and Collective Bargaining Convention. The ILO has continued
with later Conventions and backed them by the supervisory machinery
we shall note in Chapter 5.

Article 21 states that the will of the people is 'the basis of the
authority of government'. Every people has the right to choose its own
government. There should be free, secret and periodic elections on the
basis of 'universal and equal suffrage'. Everyone has 'the right to take
part in the government of his country' and 'the right of equal access
to public service in his country'. Article 22 speaks of the 'right to
social security'. Articles 23 and 24 stress the rights of labour – free
choice of employment, fair remuneration, trade unions, and, a necessary addition in modern society, 'the right to rest and leisure'.

Article 25 on the rights of the family – food, clothing, housing –
relates also to the 1959 Declaration of the Rights of the Child. Behind
Articles 26 and 27, we recognise human rights in education. 'Education
shall be free, at least in the elementary and fundamental stages', and
'elementary education shall be compulsory'. The main point of Article
27 is that 'everyone has the right freely to participate in the cultural
life of the community', surely a corollary of the previous Article that
all 'education shall be directed to the full development of the human
personality' and that 'the objective of such education is that it shall
promote understanding, tolerance and friendship among all nations,
racial, or religious groups, and shall further the activities of the United
Nations for the maintenance of peace'.

The last three Articles of the Declaration call for a new international
order based on the foregoing rights (Article 28); Article 29 stresses that
the 'general welfare in a democratic society' is sustained by the fact
that 'everyone has *duties* to the community, in which alone the free
and full development of his personality is possible'. Article 30 was
added to deter any 'State, group, or person' from employing the words
of the Declaration to defeat its objectives.

Thus, 30 years ago, mankind entered a new era with an agreed Code
of Conduct for individuals and nations alike, far surpassing the scope of
the venerable Code of Hammurabi, or the Commandments of Moses, or
the Twelve Tables of Roman Law, ever enlarging the experience and the
aspirations of 30 or more centuries. In this book, we can only focus on

a limited range of its precepts concerning working people and how these precepts have (or have not) been embodied in the rules and practices of today's 150 or so sovereign states. As we shall show later, the standards of the original Declaration have been spelled out in greater detail in both UN Covenants[1] and ILO Conventions. From the seeds of 1948 a mighty movement of global social justice has grown.

Note

1. For the texts of the relevant Articles 6 to 9 of the UN Covenant on Economic, Social and Cultural Rights, see Appendix A.

2 HOW THE ILO SYSTEM WORKS

The objectives and activities of the ILO encompass many of the rights covered by the above-mentioned International Covenant on Economic, Social and Cultural Rights. The ILO is, in fact, the Specialised Agency in the United Nations system having responsibility for social and labour questions; related especially to the right to work and to social security. It deals also with certain aspects of the right to an adequate standard of living, to family protection and to education. So it will occupy a large place in this book.

Traditionally, the ILO, to a far greater extent than other agencies, operates by way of international standards in the form of Conventions and Recommendations. Both are subject to a strict and long established constitutional procedure. This requires, for instance, that governments bring them to the attention of their national authorities, usually the legislature. Furthermore, governments must report to the ILO periodically on the measures taken to *implement* them. For ILO Conventions possess a binding character when ratified. Their ratification opens the way to a formal procedure of complaint for non-compliance by other ratifying countries. On the other hand, Recommendations do not create such legal obligations but advocate more detailed rules and are often linked to a particular Convention which they complement.

It is when we turn to the more specific standards and procedures established by the International Labour Organisation, that we come closer to the basic realities of the worker's protection under world law. In fact, 'world law' is not a misnomer in the ILO vocabulary, because eminent authorities have for decades referred to ILO Conventions as 'international legislation'.[1] But to understand this emphasis on *world* standards in the special field of labour, we must first look briefly at the historic background and some of the people and ideas that gave birth to the ILO in our time. For it would be a mistake to imagine that 'labour standards' are some newfangled notion imposed on unwilling humanity by some do-gooders in the recent past.

The principal originator of the *idea* of international labour was Daniel Le Grand, a French employer, who from 1840 to 1853 repeatedly appealed to European Governments for *joint* agreement on labour legislation as a means of eliminating economic competition. He worked on several projects for labour laws covering hours of work, rest days, night work, and unhealthy or dangerous occupations, as well as special rules for children. But Le Grand died without seeing his projects brought to fruition.

However, the idea of protecting the worker in his job found other advocates for the drafting of common international measures for the 'regulation' of labour, as it was called, and for extending the action taken by some leading industrialists concerned with the welfare of their workers. Later, the fast growing Trade Union movement began to forge international links of its own. Meanwhile, domestic laws to restrict child labour and some forms of women's work had been adopted in Britain and by several other countries.

Politicians were beginning to feel that these measures should be standardised by international agreement. The first positive initiative came in 1889 when the Swiss Federal Council sent out invitations to 13 governments to attend a conference to consider what points of labour law it would be desirable to regulate by international convention. The Swiss Federal Council, however, decided to abandon its own conference and to support a German project. So the ball was set rolling. The result was an international factory and mineworkers' conference, which opened in Berlin on 15 March 1890. It produced recommendations for the regulation of mine labour, Sunday work, child labour and the employment of women; yet no formal commitments were entered into. Other conferences followed.

Then, in November 1914, the American Federation of Labor adopted a resolution calling for 'a meeting of representatives of organised labor of the different nations to meet at the same time and place' as any peace congress to be held at the close of the War. Two years later, in 1916, a Trade Union Conference was held in Leeds, England, under the joint auspices of the British and French labour movements. This Conference moved that certain guarantees for workers, covering broadly hours of work, social security and occupational safety, should be included in the Peace Treaty. A significant point was that it also proposed the establishment of an international commission to supervise the application of those provisions and that the commission should include both workers' and employers' representatives. It was this Leeds Conference that called for the creation of a permanent international labour office. Here was the germ of the ILO as we know it today.[2]

As the First World War drew towards its end, further meetings were held which demanded that labour should be represented at the Peace Conference, and that a world conference of labour and socialism should be held simultaneously. On the initiative of the American Federation of Labor, again, a September conference adopted a series of principles which it was hoped to see included in the Peace Treaty itself, so as to constitute the foundation of social justice throughout the world. When the Peace Conference met in 1919 one of its first acts was to appoint a Commission on 'international labour legislation' to draw up proposals for inclusion in the Treaty. The Commission met under the chairmanship of the American Trade Union leader Samuel Gompers. The text it drafted became Part XIII of the Treaty of Versailles, thus creating the International Labour Organisation, as a permanent section of the League of Nations in Geneva, Switzerland. The ILO principles and structure have remained substantially the same since then.

Defining the Code

A very important Article of the Covenant of the League of Nations dealt specifically with labour rights. This Article began:

Article 23 (Social Activities)
Subject to and in accordance with the provisions of international conventions existing or hereafter to be agreed upon, the members of the League − (a) Will endeavour to secure and maintain fair and humane conditions of labour for men, women and children, both in their own countries and in all countries to which their commercial and industrial relations extend, and for that purpose will establish and maintain the necessary international organizations . . .

The ILO was envisaged by its founders primarily as an organisation for raising standards by building up a code of 'international legislation' (to accord it its widely accepted name). In the years between the two World Wars this was, in fact, the ILO's chief function, and one which it performed with conspicuous success. Despite the many new areas into which the ILO has since extended its activities, standard setting in labour and social relations retains its vital importance. These international standards take the form, as we have said, of Conventions and Recommendations. It is enough to note here that, since its establishment, a total of over 150 Conventions and close to 160 Recommendations have been adopted. Taken together, these form a world-wide Labour Code, which appears today as heavily annotated volumes of labour 'rights' in all the official languages.

  Although the ILO was the product of the social thought of the industrially developed countries of Europe and America, the objectives assigned to the new Organisation were not those of any particular society or time, for the ILO was conceived as the protector of the interests of working men and women everywhere. The universal nature of the goals set before the ILO more than a generation ago has enabled the Organisation to respond and adapt itself to the growing challenge of the developing world.

During the course of the Second World War the ILO (which had continued its basic operations in Montreal, Canada) considered the policies which it would be called upon to pursue when peace came again, and how best to co-operate with the projected United Nations Organisation. Hence, in Philadelphia in 1944, the International Labour Conference was reconvened and it hammered out a new definition of its aims and purposes. This declaration of labour rights, called the Declaration of Philadelphia, reaffirms the ILO's basic principles: namely, *that labour is not a commodity, that freedom of expression and of association are essential to progress, that poverty anywhere constitutes a danger to prosperity everywhere, and, finally, that the war on want must be carried on both within each nation and by concerted international effort.*

Seventy-Five Years Ago
December 16, 1903

NEW YORK — Two explosions in unfinished buildings in this city show that the use of dynamite as an argument in labor disputes in New York has begun. The question is whether unions representing unskilled labor should be allowed. They are often combinations for the purpose of coercing employers to yield to demands for increase in wages, reduction in hours, or whatever else subversive demands the leaders may see proper to incite their men to ask. The principle of these "labor-trusts" is coercion, and when mild methods fail, dynamite makes its appearance.
— Press item.

Some Earlier Principles

The Philadelphia Declaration confirms that 'lasting peace can be established only if it is based on social justice'. It affirms that:

(a) All human beings, irrespective of race, creed, or sex, have the right to pursue both their material well-being and their spiritual development in conditions of freedom and dignity of economic security and equal opportunity.

(b) The attainment of the conditions in which this shall be possible must constitute the central aim of national and international policy.

Perhaps today we can better appreciate the foresight of a wartime Declaration which asserted that the principles it proclaimed —

are fully applicable to all peoples everywhere and that, while the manner of their application must be determined with due regard to the stage of social and economic development reached by each people, their progressive application to peoples who are still dependent, as well as those who have already achieved self-government, is a matter of concern to the whole civilized world.

We have stressed the historic part that the 1944 Declaration played because the later edifices of both the Human Rights Covenants and the ILO Conventions concerning labour rights have been based on it. The Philadelphia Conference laid down the obligation of the ILO to achieve the following objectives in its future programmes:

(a) Full employment and the raising of standards of living;

(b) The employment of workers in the occupations in which they can have the satisfaction of giving the fullest measure of their skill and attainments and make their greatest contribution to the common well-being;

(c) Facilities for training and labour mobility;

(d) Equitable remuneration;

(e) The effective recognition of the right of collective bargaining, the co-operation of management and labour in the improvement of efficiency, and the collaboration of workers and employers in the preparation and application of economic and social measures;

(f) The extension of social security measures to provide a basic income and comprehensive medical care;

(g) Protection for the life and health of workers;

(h) Provision for child welfare and maternity protection;

(i) Adequate nutrition, housing and facilities for recreation

and culture;
(j)   Equality of educational and vocational opportunity.

It will be noticed that some of these objectives, such as adequate nutrition, child welfare, cultural facilities and education, have since become the primary responsibility of other United Nations agencies.

Four years later, the Universal Declaration (see Chapter 1) spelled out many of these aims in the following articles:

Article 22
Everyone, as a member of society, has the right to social security and is entitled to realization, through national effort and international co-operation and in accordance with the organization and resources of each State, of the economic, social and cultural rights indispensable for his dignity and the free development of his personality.

Article 23
(1) Everyone has the right to work, to free choice of employment, to just and favourable conditions of work and to protection against unemployment.

(2) Everyone, without any discrimination, has the right to equal pay for equal work.

(3) Everyone who works has the right to just and favourable remuneration ensuring for himself and his family an existence worthy of human dignity, and supplemented, if necessary, by other means of social protection.

(4) Everyone has the right to form and to join trade unions for the protection of his interests.

Article 24
Everyone has the right to rest and leisure, including reasonable limitation of working hours and periodic holidays with pay.

Article 25
(1) Everyone has the right to a standard of living adequate for the health and well-being of himself and of his family, including food, clothing, housing and medical care and necessary social services, and the right to security in the event of unemployment, sickness, disability, widowhood, old age or other lack of livelihood in circumstances beyond his control.

(2) Motherhood and childhood are entitled to special care and assistance. All children, whether born in or out of wedlock, shall enjoy the same social protection.

But it is in the field of *implementation* that the ILO will be seen, after 60 years of pioneering and experiment, as having cut new pathways in defending, rather than just defining, human rights, as we shall analyse in Part Two. The essential quasi-judicial machinery of the ILO that we shall examine contains two vital elements, namely, the importance of the Conventions and the value of the supervisory system the ILO has built over half a century of actual experience.

Each Convention is a specific legal instrument regulating some aspect of human rights or labour policy, framed as a model for national legislation. Though member countries are not bound to ratify Conventions, in accepting the ILO Constitution, they are *obliged* to bring all approved Conventions to the attention of their own legislative bodies. If a Convention is ratified, the ratifying country must report periodically to the ILO on the manner of its implementation. The total number of ratifications has today topped 4,600. It is important to remember, therefore, that the machinery so far devised for implementing UN Human Rights principles has been far surpassed by the actual working procedures of its older partner, the ILO, truly the pioneer in this wide field.

The ILO Today

Figure 1 allows us to see a little more clearly the origins and purposes of the Organisation that has played so active a part amidst the most striking series of changes since the Second World War, namely, the large-scale development of technical co-operation. For ILO efforts have been directed consistently to the preservation of basic human rights alongside these changes, above all in the improvement of living and working conditions and the promotion of full employment. However, the ILO remains essentially a standard-setting body, though today there is marked emphasis on operational programmes. The expansion of these operational programmes, particularly the World Employment Programme, has been largely responsible for decentralising responsibilities from Geneva headquarters to various regions of the world.

We cannot pursue here these pragmatic extensions of the ILO programme. To understand the dominant position of the famous Conventions, however, we must now turn to consider the central organisation in Geneva. In short, the Organisation is composed of a general assembly,

Figure 1

INTERNATIONAL LABOUR ORGANISATION

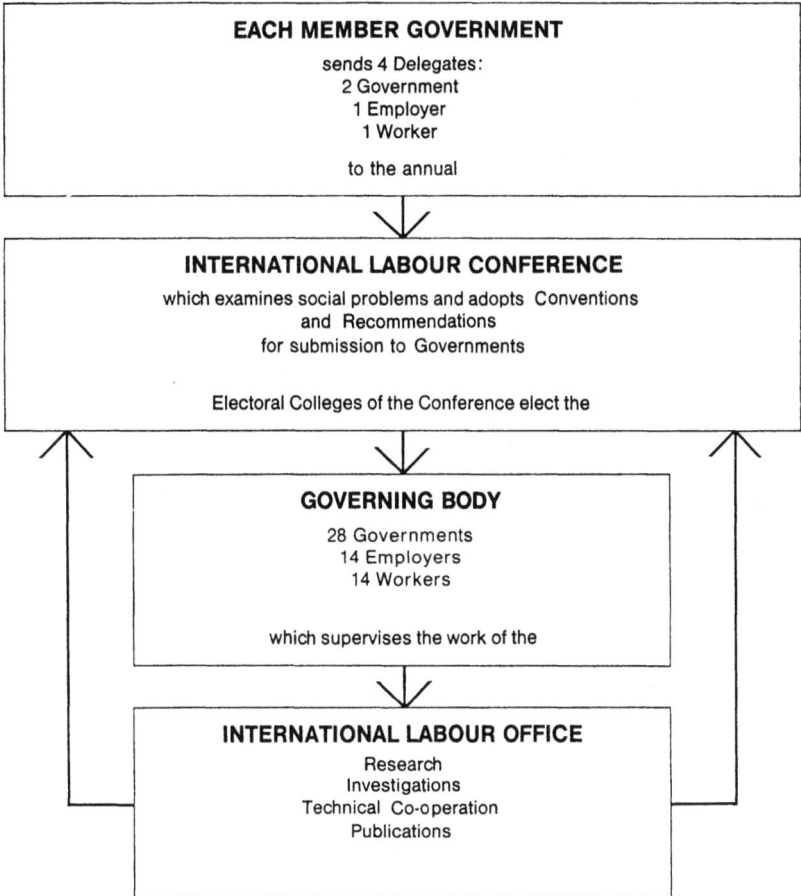

EACH MEMBER GOVERNMENT

sends 4 Delegates:
2 Government
1 Employer
1 Worker

to the annual

INTERNATIONAL LABOUR CONFERENCE

which examines social problems and adopts Conventions
and Recommendations
for submission to Governments

Electoral Colleges of the Conference elect the

GOVERNING BODY

28 Governments
14 Employers
14 Workers

which supervises the work of the

INTERNATIONAL LABOUR OFFICE

Research
Investigations
Technical Co-operation
Publications

that is, the International Labour Conference, which meets every year; an executive council, as its Governing Body; and a permanent Secretariat, which is the Office. It is the International Labour Conference that elects the Governing Body, adopts the budget, financed by contributions from member states, and actually sets international labour standards. Each national delegation to the Conference comprises two government delegates, one employers' delegate and one workers' delegate, accompanied by technical advisers. Employers' and workers' delegates have a free voice and they can, and often do, disagree with the governments and with each other.

Like the Conference, the Governing Body is tripartite and is currently composed of 56 members — 28 representing governments, 14 representing workers and 14 representing employers. The Office in Geneva prepares the documents and reports which feed the Conferences and specialised meetings of the Organisation. It engages in research and educational activities, and also issues a broad range of specialised publications. For it is a *sine qua non* of international decision-making to get the facts straight.

We must now familiarise ourselves with the successive steps that lead up to the adoption of a Convention (or Recommendation). This is a lengthy process, from the placing of an item on the agenda of the Conference to the final voting by the Conference in plenary session, where workers and employers have a fundamentally important role to play alongside governments. It is obvious that this is a very different process from establishing a United Nations Covenant, as we noted earlier. Even more so, the supervisory machinery, too, has been developed over the years to ensure that ratified Conventions are effectively implemented so that governments may comply with their obligations under the ILO Constitution.

The first step to a Convention is that, at the Governing Body's request, the Office prepares a comparative study of the laws and practices relating to the subject in the various states. This is a complicated task, not just because of the large number of member states, but also because many of the subjects covered by ILO standards are highly technical. Then, on the basis of this law-and-practice report, the Governing Body makes the final decision on whether or not to go ahead with a Convention (or Recommendation). If the answer is 'yes', an outline of a possible text is prepared. This is sent to the member states not less than a year before the start of the next session of the Conference. The governments' answers must be sent to the ILO at least eight months before the Conference meets. In preparing their answers, governments are expected to consult workers' and employers' organisations, and many of them in fact do this.

On the basis of governments' replies, the Office prepares a set of proposed conclusions, which in reality is the first draft of the proposed Convention (or Recommendation). This is sent to governments four months before the beginning of the Conference. When the Conference meets it normally appoints a tripartite committee to examine the proposals. A resultant agreed text is submitted to the full Conference, together with a resolution placing the question on the agenda of the Conference the *following* year, with a view to its adoption. After this first Conference discussion, the Office drafts a provisional text of the proposed Convention (or Recommendation) and sends it to governments within two months of the closing of the Conference. Governments have three months in which to submit amendments or make other suggestions. The Office then prepares a final report and sends it to the governments at least three months before the next session of the Conference. At that Conference, the draft is again examined by a tripartite committee and the agreed text put before the full Conference for approval. If it receives two-thirds of the votes cast it is formally adopted as an ILO Convention (or Recommendation).

Laying Down the Code

The International Labour Code, as it is called today, comprises a total of 153 Conventions and 161 Recommendations that have so far been adopted. By far the great majority of these Conventions and Recommendations can be said to relate to human rights in their widest sense, as defined in the Universal Declaration of Human Rights and the subsequent Human Rights Covenants. Thus, in addition to the Conventions which concern these fundamental human rights, that have traditionally been of paramount concern to the ILO, namely, freedom of association, freedom from forced labour, and freedom from discrimination in employment and occupation, additional 'rights' have been adopted in the fields of employment policy, vocational guidance and training, conditions of work and life, occupational safety and health, social security, industrial relations, and labour administration. Moreover, specific standards have also been adopted for the protection of special categories of workers: such as children, young persons, women or migrants, as well as to take into account the particular needs of different branches of industry: such as mining, transport or agriculture.

But with the ILO, the *adoption* of international labour rights is not an end in itself. The equally important task remains of ensuring that these standards, which represent the common ground attained by this unique 'world parliament' of government, workers' and employers' representatives, should exercise a positive influence on labour and social policies throughout the entire membership. For the ILO Constitution provides for a number of complementary procedures for monitoring the effect given to the Conventions and Recommendations when adopted. Let us look briefly at the chief of these procedures. It is in this respect, perhaps, that the ILO contribution to workers' world rights differs fundamentally from what can be called the UN approach.

A fundamental obligation is imposed on member governments to submit to the competent national authorities, within a period of 12 to 18 months after their adoption by the Conference, the texts of the Conventions (and Recommendations) and they must inform the Office of the actual measures taken to this effect. The workers' and employers' organisations, too, share the responsibility to ascertain whether their governments have complied with this obligation and what proposals they have made to implement it. This is the first step towards the implementation of ILO labour rights.

Ratification of an ILO Convention by a member state also entails a constitutional obligation to report periodically to the Office on the measures taken *to give effect* to the provisions of the Convention. The forms of report provided for this purpose call for information on the specific effect given to the requirements of the Convention. Again, representative organisations of employers and workers are given an opportunity prescribed in the Constitution to check the accuracy of the reports and to submit to the ILO any observations they deem necessary.

Now we come to a third step. A special Committee of Experts on the Application of Conventions and Recommendations is charged with the task of examining from a technical and legal point of view these reports from governments and of presenting their conclusions on the degree of compliance with ratified Conventions. This Committee is currently composed of 18 eminent persons, with high qualifications in the legal or social fields and also with an intimate knowledge of labour adminis-tration. Each annual Session of the Conference reviews the report of the Committee of Experts which is considered by a special Conference Committee where governments, employers and workers are all repre-sented. Expert examination is followed by a discussion in which govern-ment delegates of countries alleged to be in default have an opportunity of giving explanations on their own behalf. Frequently, the Commit-tee of Experts has been able to include in its report cases in which governments, responding to earlier comments by the Committee, have introduced changes into their laws and practice in order to give fuller effect to ratified Conventions.

Any employers' or workers' organisation can make a representation to the ILO to the effect that a given member state has failed to secure the effective observance of any Convention which it has ratified. The Governing Body may then communicate this representation to the government concerned for its comments. If no satisfactory comments are received within a reasonable time, the Governing Body may publish the representation and the government's reply. In doing so, the Governing Body also indicates in what respects it considers issues raised by the representation to have been satisfactorily disposed of or what further action or clarification is required. The examination is carried out by a Committee of Three, composed of three members of the Governing Body chosen from the government, employers' and workers' groups, which reports its findings to the Governing Body. We take this process further in Chapter 5.

At the Grassroots Level

There are innumerable ways in which ILO Conventions and Recommendations have changed labour laws in such matters as hours of work, weekly rest, holidays with pay, social security, employment at sea, and much else. Hundreds of examples could be quoted showing the impact of these standards on national law and practice, as well as on the working conditions of men and women in their jobs.

In Japan for many years the trade unions campaigned for the adoption of minimum wages which would permit Japan to give effect to ILO standards and make possible the ratification of the ILO Convention. Some legislation was enacted in 1958 which did not fully meet the ILO standards, so the demands for improved protection continued and in 1968 further laws were passed to eliminate these shortcomings; and this resulted in 1971 in Japan's ratifying the relevant ILO Convention. These measures led to a programme extending minimum wage protection to some 30 million workers.

Australia is another example. It ratified in 1973 the Convention on Discrimination in Employment and Occupation to ensure that a policy of non-discrimination in employment was not only declared but observed in practice. Special committees were set up both at the Federal and State levels for investigating complaints made by workers who considered that they had been the victims of discrimination in employment. In the first year of their existence these committees carefully examined some 600 cases of workers who considered that there had been discrimination inconsistent with ILO standards.

Again, a whole series of changes in recent years in labour laws of the Federal Republic of Germany have been made to ensure compliance with ILO Conventions. These changes were concerned more particularly with the minimum age for employment, entitlement to holidays with pay, and important questions of industrial safety and health and workmen's compensation, as well as working conditions in the merchant marine and on fishing vessels. Clearly, these legislative changes have made considerable improvements in the working conditions of thousands of ordinary men and women.

To give an example from the neighbouring country, the German Democratic Republic ratified recently a Convention providing for repatriation of seafarers disembarked away from their home country. Special legislation was adopted which virtually reproduced the ILO requirements so as to extend to GDR seafarers the protection provided in the Convention.

Also on the issue of itinerant workers, a court decision in France in 1975 recognised that a Spanish worker residing in France could receive workmen's compensation payments to which he would not normally have been entitled. This was because, under an ILO Convention which France had ratified, the court held that, as a result of its ratification, that particular Convention had become part of the law of France and so could be enforced by the courts.

A particularly interesting case arose when Brazil, which had not in fact ratified the ILO Convention dealing with the guarding of machinery, enacted legislation in 1967 which made it a condition for the *import* of machinery that ILO standards on guarding of machinery be complied with as protection against industrial accidents.

UN and ILO Work Together

On the legal level, there is a useful cross-fertilisation of the separate UN and ILO procedures. For example, the International Covenant on Economic, Social and Cultural Rights, which was approved by the General Assembly of the United Nations on 16 December 1966 and entered into force on 3 January 1976, contains a number of provisions dealing with matters of direct concern to the ILO. The chief of these are: Article 6 (the right to work); Article 7 (the right to just and favourable conditions of work); Article 8 (trade union rights); and Article 9 (the right to social security).[3]

The International Labour Conference has long expressed the Organisation's readiness to play its full part in ensuring the implementation of the provisions of the UN's International Covenants. In fact, in 1967, the Conference adopted a resolution inviting member states of the ILO to consider early ratification or accession to the Covenants and also to ratify and implement ILO Conventions in the same field. The Governing Body undertook a comparative study of the provisions of the Covenants and of the labour Conventions (and Recommendations) so far adopted, so as to assess how the ILO could best assist in promoting the protection of human rights.

This joint reporting system does not call for detailed analysis here, but it should be recalled that, in accordance with Article 16 of the UN Covenant, states Parties are required to report to the Economic and Social Council on the measures that they have adopted and the progress made in achieving the observance of rights recognised in the Covenant. The Economic and Social Council has also made arrangements with the ILO for reporting by them on progress made in achieving observance of the provisions of the Covenant falling within the scope of ILO activities. The 56 states having so far ratified or acceded to the Covenant are all Members of the ILO.

This is not merely a theoretical operation. Typical of this close relationship, a point of substance arises in relation to Article 7, which concerns measures to ensure fair wages to all workers. Detailed information would appear desirable concerning the criteria used in the various countries for determining the 'fairness' of wages, so as to meet the requirements of the Covenant. More precise indications concerning the scope of existing wage-fixing measures would have to show whether the enjoyment of the right to fair wages is being ensured to workers generally. Again, we notice that Article 8 of the Covenant deals with trade union rights, a subject of fundamental concern to the ILO.

The most relevant ILO Convention in this field, as we have seen, is No. 87, the Freedom of Association and Protection of the Right to Organise Convention 1948, to which reference is actually made in Article 8. In some respects the rights provided for in Article 8 of the Covenant are formulated in more general terms than those guaranteed by Convention No. 87. While it is useful to distinguish between obligations under the Covenant and the Convention, respectively, the guarantees provided in the Covenant are very important, such as Article 8(3):

Nothing in this Article shall authorise States Parties to the International Labour Organisation Convention of 1948 concerning freedom of association and protection of the right to organise to take legislative measures which would prejudice, or apply the law in such a manner as would prejudice, the guarantees provided for in that Convention.

For the first time, in 1978, the ILO's Committee of Experts on the Application of Conventions and Recommendations reported to the United Nations on progress in putting into effect such guarantees on labour matters. This marked the beginning of a joint UN-ILO action in the field of labour rights, aimed at strengthening the rights guaranteed by the Covenant on Economic, Social and Cultural Rights. This Covenant entered into force on 3 January 1976 and was later ratified by 56 states. So the Specialised Agencies, including the ILO, have been given a special role, within the scope of the Agencies.

Although this is a somewhat technical subject, and may not seem very important to the layman, the recently appointed Human Rights Committee, set up under the International Covenant on Civil and Political Rights and its Protocol that deals with individual complaints, has been reluctant, up to this point, to receive information direct from the Specialised Agencies, such as the ILO, falling within the field of their activities and within the scope of the Committee's work. Since the ILO would normally be in a position to contribute valuable insights to the Committee's consideration of particular labour rights, this reluctance appears to be another instance where sovereign states seek to hide behind the procedure of a UN technical body, rather than 'face the music'. Perhaps wiser counsels will prevail as the Committee develops its authority?

It should be noted that rights concerning workers covered by the International Covenant on Economic, Social and Cultural Rights need only be achieved progressively by the states Parties. On trade union rights, however, the Covenant requires states Parties to undertake to ensure them as immediate obligations. Workers' rights in such fields as working conditions 'require continuing efforts to achieve a progressive raising of standards of welfare'. The realisation of trade union rights, on the other hand, 'is not dependent on availability of resources, but could represent an important contribution to the harnessing of the energies and support of the productive forces in society to the development process'. These observations on progress in putting into effect the Covenant's guarantees on labour were made in 1979 by the Committee of Experts on the Application of Conventions and Recommendations and sent to the UN's Economic and Social Council as part of the new procedure in monitoring observance of the UN Covenant's provisions.

Meantime, in evaluating the implementation of the *Covenant*, the UN Committee is competent to draw for its general findings on the application of the ILO *Conventions*. It may be too early to draw conclusions at this stage, but the Committee has already stressed the need for more information on *actual steps taken* by states to implement a legally recognised right to work, and on how far this right has been *realised in practice*. It has also asked for more detailed information on measures to ensure 'fair wages' for all workers. Slowly but surely, governments are beginning to yield their claims of absolute sovereignty to the new instruments of international social justice described in this chapter.

Notes

1. cf. Manley O. Hudson, *International Legislation* (Carnegie Foundation, 1929).
2. This development is told in greater detail in the author's *Broken Star, the Story of the League of Nations* (Christopher Davies, 1978).
3. For the relevant texts of these four Articles, see Appendix A.

3 THE EUROPEAN COMMISSION

Regional Commissions concerning workers' rights have been playing a significant role since the Second World War; but only one of them — by far the most active one — can be detailed in this chapter. Passing notice, however, should be taken of the first regional organisation to be created at the inter-governmental level, namely, the Organisation of American States (OAS), which became also the first regional organisation to concern itself with questions of human rights. Another much later one was the League of Arab States; and steps have been taken recently, too, to set up a human rights procedure under the Organisation of African Unity (OAU).

In the initial decades of its existence, OAS dealt mostly with civil and political rights, but later directed its attention to the new fields of economic, social and cultural rights. Here, the American Declaration of the Rights and Duties of Man (1948) and the Inter-American Charter of Social Guarantees (also adopted by OAS in 1948) are still models to the Western world. Labour is described as a 'social function' which requires special protection. Workers' rights, which may not be renounced, include the free choice and fair conditions of employment and vocational guidance. Employment should provide guarantees of stability, with due regard to the nature of the work, and arbitrary dismissals give the right to indemnification. Workers should have the right to a compulsory system of social security, designed to attain the elimination of the hazards that might deprive wage-earners of the means of support for themselves and their dependants and the means of support in the case of termination or interruption of their occupational activity. Moreover, workers should have the right to share in an equitable distribution of the national well-being and to obtain food, clothing and housing at reasonable prices. A Commission was established by OAS to implement these principles.

We must pass immediately, however, to consider the more advanced and sophisticated machinery at the disposal of the European community. At the European regional level, the organisation dealing with the protection of human rights is the Council of Europe, which consists of 18 member states. Its 1949 Statute provides that every member of the Council must accept the principles of the rule of law and the enjoyment of human rights and fundamental freedoms by all persons within its jurisdiction.

Under the Council's sponsorship, the Convention for the Protection of Human Rights and Fundamental Freedoms was concluded in 1950 and has since been ratified by 18 states. Though mainly devoted to civil and political rights, it also covers some economic, social and cultural rights, notably in prohibiting forced labour and discrimination 'on any ground' and in affirming the right of everyone to enjoy freedom of association, 'including the right to form and join trade unions for the protection of his interests'.

The rights contained in the European Convention and in its First and Fourth Protocols are based, in part, on the Universal Declaration of Human Rights; but the Convention also contains elaborate implementation procedures, which are described in detail below. Under the terms of the Convention, a Commission and Court of Human Rights have been set up, which, together with the Committee of Ministers of the Council of Europe (a political body), are responsible for the implementation of the provisions of the Convention. Thus, depending on which of these organs handles a particular case, three types of remedies are possible: conciliatory, if the Commission secures a friendly settlement between the parties; judicial, if the case is brought before the Court; quasi-judicial, if decided by the Committee of Ministers.

The following are among the 20 rights guaranteed by the Convention and the First and Fourth Protocols: viz. the right to life; freedom from torture and from inhuman treatment or punishment; freedom from slavery and servitude; the right to liberty and security of person; the right to a fair trial; freedom of expression; and freedom of assembly and association.

How the Procedure Works

The Commission consists of a number of independent members, equal to the number of the contracting parties, elected by the Committee of Ministers. It may receive complaints from any contracting party and petitions from any person, group or non-governmental organisation, provided the government concerned recognises the Commission's competence. The Commission determines the facts alleged in the complaint or petition and attempts to bring about a friendly settlement of the dispute. If it fails, it draws up a report stating its opinion on the validity of the case and submits it to the Committee of Ministers and to the States concerned. If the question is not referred to the Court within three months, the Committee of Ministers must decide whether there has been violation of the Convention, prescribe a time-limit for corrective measures and, if none are taken, publish a report.

The Court consists of a number of judges equal to that of the members of the Council of Europe. It is competent to deal with all cases relative to the application of the Convention, but only after the efforts of the Commission to achieve a friendly settlement have failed. Any member of the Council may declare that it accepts as compulsory the Court's jurisdiction. Where such compulsory jurisdiction has been recognised, the Court's judgement is final. A further implementation is offered by Article 13 of the Convention, which states: 'Everyone whose rights and freedoms as set forth in this Convention are violated shall have an effective remedy before a *national* authority, notwithstanding that the violation has been committed by persons acting in an official capacity.' This provision is important because not only does it ensure access to national courts, it also precludes the excuse that the violation has been committed in an official capacity.

European Social Charter

Only a few economic, social and cultural rights, as it happens, have been dealt with in the Convention, because the Council of Europe takes the view that such rights essentially belong to a separate instrument. This instrument, the European Social Charter, was signed in 1961. The economic and social rights protected and realised are those already listed in the International Covenant on Economic, Social and Cultural Rights. In addition, the right to vocational guidance and training, the right of everyone to engage in lucrative occupations and the right to protection of migrant workers are also listed in the Charter.

Perhaps we might revert to what was stated in our last chapter about the right to organise, enshrined in the 1948 ILO Convention on Freedom of Association and Protection of the Right to Organise. Although an identical provision is not found in the European Convention, several interesting cases have recently been filed which have made legal history. The first of these was *Belgian National Police Union* v. *Belgium,* arising from an Act of 1961 introducing various changes affecting the staff structures, conditions of recruitment and salary scales of provincial and communal employees in that country. A trade unions' advisory committee was set up at the Ministry of the Interior for this purpose, but the only union representatives thereon were those of the three main political unions in Belgium. The National Police Union objected, claiming that, as a national federation of local police associations, it should be accepted as representative of its members as required by the ILO Convention, since, to allow individuals to join a union but then to refuse to negotiate with it, constituted a restricted notion of trade union freedom. The Commission adopted its report in May 1974 and reached the conclusion that no violation had occurred, but referred the case to the Court of Human Rights in view of the importance of the issues raised. On 27 October 1975, the Court confirmed the Commission's conclusion.

On the negative side, similar issues were raised in a Swedish case: *Swedish Pilots' Association* v. *Sweden*. The Pilots' Association, which represented the majority of all Swedish pilots, was affiliated to one of the major Swedish labour organisations and sought to negotiate separately with the National Collective Bargaining Office (SAV). The latter refused to do so as its policy was to negotiate only with the four major labour organisations in Sweden. But this application was declared inadmissible in 1972 for failure to comply with a six-months rule contained in Article 26 of the European Convention.

These two cases are cited to stress, first, that the European Convention is a living reality in Western Europe and, second, that a case law is developing which is establishing a texture of European social 'legislation'. Contributing continually to this end is the Social Charter that contains a dynamic element which enables it to adjust itself to social evolution in European countries and so ensure that social progress is one of the aims implemented by the Council of Europe. Like the UN Covenants on Human Rights, the Social Charter is not a simple declaration of intent, but a legal instrument for ensuring the effective enjoyment of recognised rights. The first Part of the Charter contains the 19 aims that the Contracting Parties have decided to pursue; the second Part consists of 19 articles corresponding to them. It is in this second Part, in Article 6 on 'the right to bargain collectively', that the right to strike is recognised for the first time in an *international* instrument.

The Social Charter also sets up machinery for the supervision of its application. But in view of the different nature of the rights recognised, this is not legal machinery, as in the case of the UN Covenant on Human Rights. It is based rather on the system in force within the International Labour Organisation, which has always been the pioneer in the protection of workers' rights. But the Charter does provide that the European Consultative Assembly or Parliament shall be called upon to express its opinion. The fact that the parliamentary organ of the Council holds a 'watching brief' over the social policy of their neighbours enables European public opinion to exert pressure on governmental bodies to ensure that the Charter is applied in all the countries concerned.

Since there was bound to be a certain overlapping among the 19 aforementioned aims contained in the Charter, we can best conclude this chapter by listing below the dozen most substantial ones that the Contracting Parties have accepted as the aims of their national policy:

Everyone shall have the opportunity to earn his living in an occupation freely entered upon.

All workers have the right to safe and healthy working conditions.

All workers have the right to a fair remuneration sufficient for a decent standard of living for themselves and their families.

All workers and employers have the right to freedom of association in national or international organisations for the protection of their economic and social interests.

All workers and employers have the right to bargain collectively.

Children and young persons have the right to a special protection against the physical and moral hazards to which they are exposed.

Employed women, in case of maternity, and other employed women as appropriate, have the right to a special protection in their work.

Everyone has the right to appropriate facilities for vocational training.

All workers and their dependants have the right to social security. Everyone has the right to benefit from social welfare services.

Disabled persons have the right to vocational training, rehabilitation and resettlement, whatever the origin and nature of their disability.

The family as a fundamental unit of society has the right to appropriate social, legal and economic protection to ensure its full development.

The nationals of any one of the Contracting Parties have the right to engage in any gainful occupation in the territory of any one of the others on a footing of equality with the nationals of the latter.

Part Two

DEALING WITH COMPLAINTS

4 THE UN COVENANTS

Article 55 of the United Nations Charter makes it a duty for all UN members to 'promote . . . higher standards of living, full employment and conditions of economic and social progress and development', as well as 'universal respect for, and observance of, human rights and fundamental freedoms for all without distinction as to race, sex, language, or religion'. Under Article 56, 'All Members pledge themselves to take joint and separate action in co-operation with the Organization for the achievement of the purposes set forth in Article 55'.

These two provisions are the foundation upon which all subsequent action in this field rests. They give to the obligation of Member States the character of a rule of international law. At its first session, the General Assembly assigned to the Commission on Human Rights the task of undertaking the 'formulation of an international bill of rights'. This instrument eventually took the form of the Universal Declaration, that we summarised in Chapter 1, and of two International Covenants: the Covenant on Economic, Social and Cultural Rights and the Covenant on Civil and Political Rights, the latter with an Optional Protocol.

In view of the enormous moral authority of the Declaration, it may be looked upon as more of a legal document nowadays than when it was adopted, in regard to the 'priorities' of life in different regions of the world. Members of the UN can no longer treat these priorities with contempt, even if they have not been formally incorporated in their domestic laws. The Declaration has, fortunately, inspired the new or revised constitutions of many countries of the world and been included in the normal legislation of many others.

As stated above, the Covenant on Economic, Social and Cultural Rights provides the immediate basis for action at the international level, as well as for the translation of its standards into national reality. It is indeed one of the most important international instruments adopted by the United Nations. Its only drawback is that in less developed countries its provisions can only be implemented progressively, according to the level of their development and the size of their population. It is probably for that reason that most of these countries have found it difficult to meet the global obligations in respect of all the rights provided for. The Covenant has, however, acted as a catalyst in developing *national consciousness* on such principles as *the right to*

work, and more specifically the right to free choice of employment,
to just and favourable conditions of work, to protection against unemployment, to equal pay for equal work, to rest, leisure and periodic holidays with pay; and, not least, the right to form trade unions
and to join trade unions of one's choice, as well as the right to strike.

The permanent UN organs concerned with the formulation of these
economic, social and cultural standards include the General Assembly
and the Economic and Social Council (ECOSOC) and some of its
subsidiary bodies, notably the Commission on Human Rights and the
Commission on the Status of Women. The General Assembly may
discuss and make recommendations on any matters within the scope
of the Charter. Under Article 13, it is one of its functions to initiate
studies and make recommendations for assisting in the realisation of
human rights. And under Article 22, the General Assembly 'may
establish such subsidiary organs as it deems necessary for the performance of its functions'. Among these organs, the United Nations
Children's Fund, the United Nations Relief and Works Agency for
Palestine Refugees in the Near East, and the Office of the United
Nations High Commissioner for Refugees are especially concerned
with economic, social and cultural rights.

At its first session, in 1947, the Commission on Human Rights
established a permanent Sub-Commission on Prevention of Discrimination and Protection of Minorities. Its terms of reference are to undertake studies and to make recommendations to the Commission on
Human Rights concerning the prevention of discrimination of any kind
and the protection of racial, national, religious and linguistic minorities. This Sub-Commission is composed of 26 persons selected by the
Commission to serve, normally for three years, in their capacity as
individuals and not as representatives of states. It meets annually for
three weeks.

The Sub-Commission frequently appoints, from among its own
members, special rapporteurs to prepare reports on particular aspects
of discrimination, such as discrimination in education, discrimination
in religious rights and practices, as well as in political rights and the
right of everyone to leave any country, including his own. Studies
carried out by special rapporteurs provide the basis for the preparation
of draft instruments or draft resolutions. They are also circulated to
governments.

The parallel Commission on the Status of Women plays an important part in the realisation of economic, social and cultural rights.
Initially a sub-commission of the Commission on Human Rights, it

was given in 1946 the status of a functional commission, composed of 32 representatives of states Members, selected by the Council on the basis of an equitable geographical distribution, and meets once every two years.

In brief, items concerning economic, social and cultural rights originate for the most part in reports of ECOSOC and of the Secretary-General. They are referred to the Assembly's Third Committee, responsible for social, humanitarian and cultural questions. Not least, on the basis of Article 71, the Council may make 'arrangements for consultation with non-governmental organizations which are concerned with matters within its competence'. So this consultative relationship relates to economic, social and cultural rights.

ECOSOC established on 16 February 1946 the aforementioned Commission on Human Rights, with the task of submitting proposals, recommendations and reports to the Council regarding such matters as:

(a) International Declarations or Conventions on civil liberties, the Status of Women and Freedom of Information;
(b) The protection of minorities;
(c) The prevention of discrimination on grounds of race, sex, language or religion.

The Commission is composed of one representative from each of 32 states Members selected for three years by the Council on the basis of an equitable geographical representation. It meets once a year, reports to the Council, and may establish subsidiary bodies either on a permanent or *ad hoc* basis.

Machinery on Complaints

Thus, the mechanism provided in the UN system for ascertaining the extent to which international instruments on economic, social and cultural rights are *applied* is entrusted to the Commission on Human Rights and, via ECOSOC, to the General Assembly itself. The implementation process devised in the Economic, Social and Cultural Covenant requires states Parties to report on the measures taken to achieve its objectives. Reports are furnished in stages, as determined by ECOSOC, and may indicate any difficulties that affect the fulfilment of obligations assumed under the Covenant. The Council may refer the reports to the Commission on Human Rights for study and general recommendations. From time to time, the Council may also submit to the General Assembly recommendations on the measures taken and the progress achieved in the rights proclaimed in the Covenant.

The Economic and Social Council initiated in 1959 a 'periodic reporting system' under which states Members are invited to supply information on human rights and fundamental freedoms in territories subject to their jurisdiction. Non-governmental organisations in consultative status with ECOSOC may also present objective information on any of the topics under debate. This reporting system is not only a source of information but it may also provide an extra incentive to governments to protect the rights in question and to implement the principles set forth in the Universal Declaration.

In 1970 the Economic and Social Council laid down in Resolution 1503 a procedure for dealing with violations. Under this earlier procedure, there are three stages. First, the Sub-Commission on Prevention of Discrimination and Protection of Minorities is authorised to appoint a Working Group —

> to consider all communications, including replies of governments thereon...with a view to bringing to the attention of the Sub-Commission those communications, together with the replies of Governments, if any, which appear to reveal a consistent pattern of gross and reliably-attested violations of human rights and fundamental freedoms.

A large number of complaints have reached this Working Group, whose annual sessions are naturally held in private. Second, the Sub-Commission considers these communications and any replies of governments 'with a view to determining whether to refer to the Commission on Human Rights particular situations which appear to reveal *a consistent pattern* of gross violations of human rights'. Third, the Commission goes on to determine: (a) whether it requires a thorough study by the Commission, or (b) whether it may be the subject of an investigation by an *ad hoc* committee appointed by the Commission.

But this latter step can only be taken with the express consent of the state concerned and conducted in constant co-operation with that state. Admissible communications (that is, complaints) may originate from individuals or groups who are victims of violations, persons having direct knowledge of violations, or non-governmental organisations (not politically motivated) having direct knowledge of such violations. This earlier procedure came into operation for the first time in 1972, when the Working Group singled out complaints relating to three countries: Greece, Iran and Portugal.

The dossier of complaints in the case of Greece, for example, included a large number of personal affidavits by individuals who had been subjected to arbitrary arrest and detention, torture or cruel or inhuman treatment, and by persons who had been denied fair trials and their right to freedom of opinion, peaceful assembly and association, or deprived of their nationality, and who had also been prevented from expressing their will in genuine elections. Even with inevitable bureaucratic delays and the obstruction of certain governments, this earlier procedure nevertheless constituted a landmark in the history of the implementation of human rights. For the first time, there was a United Nations procedure under which private individuals and non-governmental organisations, as well as governments, could raise complaints about violations of human rights within a state and have those complaints investigated outside it by an impartial international body.

The 'Resolution 1503' procedure, as it is called, is universal in its application; but another procedure under the political Covenant will apply only in respect of those states which have made declarations under Article 41 (relating to complaints by other states) or which have signed the Optional Protocol (relating to complaints by individuals). This, a new Committee of 18 experts, which began its career early in 1977, is still in a pioneering stage. It is an independent body, serviced by the UN Secretariat. It was set up under the International Covenant on Civil and Political Rights after the Covenant entered into force on 23 March 1976, to examine reports by states on their implementation of the Covenant. Under the optional provisions of that Covenant it may consider communications from a state that is party to the Covenant which considers that *another* state party is not fulfilling its Covenant obligations.

Fifty-five countries have ratified the Covenant, and 21 have ratified the Optional Protocol, which has also come into force. The provisions concerning one state's complaints of violations by another have been accepted so far by ten states, and became effective in March 1979 when ten states in all had accepted the procedures. Meetings of the Committee are in public, but private meetings will be held when the Committee is considering communications from individuals.

After studying the reports submitted by each state, the Committee is authorised to send such general comments as it considers appropriate to the states who, in turn, may submit their observations on any comments made. The Committee will then transmit its comments to ECOSOC. On the basis of these reports, a permanent dialogue is expected to develop between the expert representatives of the international community, chosen to sit on this Committee, and the states Parties. It can be noted that among the communist countries which have ratified or adhered to the Covenant are Bulgaria, Byelorussia, Czechoslovakia, East Germany, Hungary, Mongolia, Poland, Romania, the Ukraine, the USSR and Yugoslavia.

Individual complaints will obviously assume a considerable place in the Committee's programme as time goes on, from individuals who claim 'to be victims of a violation of a right set forth in the Covenant by states who have accepted the Optional Protocol'. The states who have done so are: Barbados, Canada, Colombia, Costa Rica, Denmark, Dominican Republic, Ecuador, Finland, Italy, Jamaica, Madagascar, Mauritius, Netherlands, Norway, Panama, Senegal, Surinam, Sweden, Uruguay, Venezuela, and Zaire. The Committee cannot receive a complaint against a state *not* a party to the Optional Protocol, nor can it consider communications which are anonymous or which abuse the right of submission. Moreover, all available domestic remedies must have been exhausted.

Labour Rights protected by the Covenant include the right to life (Article 6); the prohibition of degrading treatment or punishment (Article 7); the prohibition of slavery and forced labour (Article 8) and arbitrary arrest or detention (Article 9), and others. The Committee submits to the General Assembly an annual report of its activities. Thus, a double procedure is evolving today within the UN system. Although limited at present to a few states, it promises to grow into one of the main organs of international justice as more states adopt the Covenant and its Protocol. It should be recalled how very recently *any* official procedure had been devised for Governments to listen collectively to complaints from individuals.

Working Groups

As will be seen from further examples selected below, Human Rights Working Groups (whether permanent or *ad hoc*) provide some varied food for thought in spite of the fact that, in action, they have only advisory functions, either with the Commission itself or ECOSOC. They possess no authority of their own except to investigate the facts and, sometimes, recommend action.

We have selected at random three current topics which differ widely from each other in scope, subject matter and geographical position, namely (a) household slavery and child labour; (b) cheap labour by compulsion; and (c) migrant workers.

Our first example is exhibited in an episode that occurred at a

Working Group meeting of the Sub-Commission on Minorities in
August 1977. This body is the five-member Expert Working Group on
Slavery that received information from the Anti-Slavery Society of
London concerning alleged 'household slavery', involving two United
Nations officials stationed in New York. The members of this Group
are not government appointees, but independent persons selected
because of their special knowledge. They sit in public session, and their
reports go to the higher bodies, and thus on to the General Assembly
itself, so world-wide publicity is assured.

This Working Group discussed on this occasion the evidence presented to it, though names of the parties were not given. The spokesman of the Anti-Slavery Society gave evidence that women employees
of the officials designated were required to work long hours without
vacation, were prevented from going out or even answering the telephone, and were subject to threats of deportation. Payment of wages
was also delayed. Members were divided on several points as to what
action to take, but as a summary of the discussion was made available
for Secretary-General Kurt Waldheim and, of course, press reports
were forthcoming, *The Times* and other leading newspapers were able
to present the allegations to the public. Public opinion can become one
of the most powerful weapons in the fight for individual rights, as
happened in this particular case.

It should be noted that in this case a voluntary society, through
channels provided by the UN system, could reach a wide public and so
stimulate protective action by the appropriate legal machinery. A suit
was presented to the US Courts, based on the international law of
Human Rights, as contained in the 1956 Supplementary Convention
on the Abolition of Slavery, the Slave Trade, and Institutions and
Practices Similar to Slavery, which, allegedly, had been violated.

Child labour, again, and even the sale of children, has long been a
matter for United Nations enquiry and action. In fact, at its most
recent session the same Working Group gave a major part of its examination to reports concerned with bonded labour in India, child labour
in Morocco's carpet industry, and the problems of rural workers in
Guatemala.

According to an investigation of the Anti-Slavery Society on
Guatemala, for instance, landowners and their labour contractors
'continue to use illegal and coercive means, including violence and
induced indebtedness, to secure a cheap labour force on their commercial farms'. There was also evidence that landowners and their labour
contractors 'had deliberately opposed development programmes by

which the rural poor might realise their economic and social rights',
and that landowners had frequently 'resorted to threats and violence
in order to achieve these ends'. The investigation concluded that
Guatemala's military rulers (who are themselves owners of large farms
in the disputed areas) have consistently used the police and military
'to the detriment of the interests of the rural poor and indigenous
peoples'. An added point was that the granting of exploitation concessions to external transnational companies had exacerbated the
existing tensions, and had led to the escalation of violence and to
deterioration in the living and working conditions of Guatemala's
rural poor.

It was in line with the procedures explained in our next chapter that
some Group members felt that a possible course of action would be for
Guatemala to accept those ILO Conventions concerning tribal popula-
tions and implement other Conventions that it has already ratified. The
United Nations itself could also consider economic aid and assistance to
help solve the problems arising in extremely poor rural areas where
peasants might suffer conditions similar to slavery.

The Group members also pointed out that debt bondage occurs when
a person pledges his services in lieu of repayment of a debt, and that, if
his services do not go towards liquidation of the debt and the length of
service is not fixed, then the situation becomes a subtle form of slavery.
The Anti-Slavery Society went down to fundamentals in asserting: 'It
may be that debt-bondage will only cease when the rural poor organise
themselves and become a significant political force.' The Society, therefore, suggested that United Nations Specialised Agencies, especially ILO
and FAO, dealing with areas where it existed, should consider the
desirability of specific action to combat debt-bondage. It also proposed
that the ILO be urged to assist national institutions (such as the Indian
National Labour Institute) to carry out detailed studies of bonded
labour and of policies to combat it.

Finally, measures to improve the lot of migrant workers and to
ensure their human rights were discussed by another Working Group of
the Commission at a one-week session in December 1978 at the Palais
des Nations in Geneva. This Group was open to all Member States, and
was set up to advise the Human Rights Commission. As a result, a set of
proposals to improve the employment situation of migrant workers and
their families was approved. Thirty-nine States participated in the
deliberations, including the host countries and countries of origin of
migrant workers.

The Working Group proposed that host countries be invited to assure migrant workers and their families equality of treatment in the field of labour, particularly concerning economic and social rights, living and working conditions, wages, and the right of association; as well as to take steps to promote the family life of migrant workers, through re-unification of their families; and, above all, to give special attention to the situation of children of migrant workers, and set up the appropriate machinery to assure them a *bi-cultural* education, including access to the teaching of their mother tongue and culture.

Governments of countries of origin were invited to inform migrant workers of their rights and obligations *before* they left home; and all States were asked to ensure that the human rights of migrant workers were safeguarded under their domestic laws. Bilateral and multilateral agreements were desirable to resolve problems of migrant workers and facilitate their reintegration in their countries of origin. Questions of protecting children of migrant workers against all forms of discrimination were to be given priority and measures to aid their adaptation to the culture of the host country were urgently needed. Violations of human rights of migrant workers, resulting from illicit traffic in such workers, were to be followed up by the Human Rights Commission. Moreover, the Commission was advised to pay special attention to promoting the reunion of families of migrant workers, and to the protection of their children against discrimination in education and other fields.

The question has been raised several times in the foregoing discussion as to whether the UN system — admittedly still in a formative stage — provides the best of all possible worlds for human rights protection, when it comes to workers' rights in their jobs. More than one authority in this field has urged that UN procedure should be shaped, as it develops, more closely to the ILO pattern. It was on this possibility that the late US Supreme Court Justice Earl Warren had this to say — and his wise words might well provide a suitable introduction to our next chapter:

> For the past three years I have had the good fortune to be associated with a judicial review panel of the ILO. I have been impressed by the extent to which the basic features of effective implementation are built into the constitutional structure of the ILO — fact dealing, exposure, conciliation, and adjudication. The handling of complaints, which is the heart of meaningful enforcement of human rights, has been carefully structured in a precise procedural manner. What is still more important, there is a record demonstrating that

these arrangements have produced concrete results. Though there may be limits to the use of ILO as a precedent, there is experience there that can be applied effectively to the entire range of human rights concerns.

5 MISSIONS AND INQUIRIES

The intimate link between the principles of the Human Rights Declaration and the working practices of the International Labour Organisation has been well expressed by Francis Blanchard, ILO Director-General, in the following words:

> Through its Conventions and Recommendations, the ILO has played its part in providing a clearer definition of the rights embodied in the Declaration. It has expanded earlier standards relating to forced labour and trade union rights and adopted such major new instruments as the Conventions dealing with discrimination in employment, equal pay, employment policy, human resources development and migrant workers. The total number of ratifications of ILO Conventions today is five times greater than it was when the Declaration was adopted. Moreover, through its operational activities, the ILO has also helped member States to work towards the realisation of the economic and social rights proclaimed in the Declaration.
>
> The Organisation has continuously sought to extend and perfect its supervisory procedures for implementing its standards far beyond what the UN itself has so far been able to achieve. It has done this by measures such as direct contacts with member States, regular reviews of problems of ratification and application of Conventions, the establishment of special procedures for the protection of trade union rights, and the use of constitutional complaints procedures.

The unique strength of the ILO, which brings it so close to the needs of workers throughout the world, is the tripartite principle on which the Organisation is based. Whereas in all the other UN organisations policies are devised and decisions taken by governments alone, in the ILO workers and employers take an equal part along with governments in all decision-making procedures. The formulation of international standards in the form of Conventions or Recommendations is supported by the development of international supervisory machinery aimed at securing implementation of these standards. These include special complaints procedures to investigate alleged violations of ILO standards.

Setting the standards is not enough. Their enforcement is clearly a vital procedure. So reports must be submitted by the governments on the way in which they are giving effect to ratified Conventions and dealing with Recommendations, and these are carefully examined by a special Committee of International Experts. This Committee prepares a report of its own for submission to the annual International Labour Conference. Then, a tripartite Conference Committee (governments, employers and workers) examines both the information received from governments and the report of the international experts. It can invite representatives of governments to appear before it to answer specific criticisms by the experts. Meetings of this Conference Committee are open to the public and its report to the plenary Conference is a public document. Experience has shown that governments are usually anxious to avoid being criticised in the Committee's report. Once again, public opinion becomes an effective means of ensuring that governments live up to their pledges.

The ILO's enforcement machinery provides for a government to complain if it believes that another government is not living up to a Convention which both have ratified. Complaints may also originate with the ILO's Governing Body or with a Conference delegate. The Governing Body may then appoint a Commission of Inquiry. Its report is published, and the government concerned has then to decide whether to accept the Commission's findings or to appeal to the International Court of Justice at The Hague. If a government fails to carry out any recommendations that have been made either by the Commission of Inquiry or based on decisions by the World Court, the Governing Body may then make recommendations to the Conference on steps to ensure compliance.

Thus, it will be observed that the ILO, within its special competence specifically in workers' rights, has already gone a long way in solving one of the most crucial and difficult problems involved in establishing world-wide standards. It has managed to combine the precision necessary for formulating an international legal instrument with the flexibility essential for its application in countries of vastly different social structures and degrees of economic development.

Probably no action undertaken by the ILO over its 60 years of existence has had a more profound impact on social and labour legislation, and consequently on the conditions of work and life of the working people in numerous countries, than this combination of standard-setting and supervisory activities.

Dealing with Complaints

The procedure for dealing with specific complaints is more elaborate than the representations by non-governmental bodies mentioned earlier. Any member *state* may file a complaint with the ILO if it is not satisfied that another member state is observing any Convention which both have ratified. The Governing Body can also act on receiving a complaint from any delegate – government, employer or worker. The Governing Body may appoint an independent Commission of Inquiry to look into any such case. If a government rejects the conclusions arrived at from such a Commission of Inquiry, it is entitled to refer the complaint to the International Court of Justice. The Court can affirm, vary or reverse the Commission's recommendations, and its decision is final.

In practice, however, no government has yet pursued any matter as far as the Court. This is certainly due to the parties' confidence in the objectivity which the investigating bodies display in discharging their responsibilities. The Commissions of Inquiry are composed of three independent persons and they follow a quasi-judicial procedure, involving examination of issues of fact and law. They call for oral and documentary evidence from the parties and they have also extended invitations to neighbouring countries to submit evidence. Witnesses may be heard at the request of the parties or of the Commission itself.

What sort of complaints have so far been examined by a Commission of Inquiry? They have included forced labour in Portuguese African territories and in Liberia, freedom of association in Greece, and the non-observance by Chile of the Conventions on discrimination in employment and hours of work. Moreover, in the cases of the Portuguese African territories and Chile, the Commission has conducted on-the-spot investigations. In each of the aforementioned cases, the Commission of Inquiry findings have been accepted by the Government concerned, and in each case important legislative or other reforms were actually being adopted while proceedings were pending or subsequently. A total of ten such representations have so far been investigated, while Commissions of Inquiry have examined only four cases. The fact that these procedures have not been used often is due probably to the fact that the ILO's regular supervisory machinery, based on the examination by the Committee of Experts, meets most situations.[1] It should not be overlooked that both employers' and workers' organisations can play an important role by submitting comments on the reports presented by their own governments. In fact, the active participation of these organisations in the supervisory process is often preferable to the more formal procedures.

When serious disagreements occur on the application of ratified Conventions dealing with fundamental human rights and sometimes in a delicate political context, the ILO has at its disposal procedures offering impartial and meticulous examination, so as to give the parties the confidence that is necessary if they are to co-operate in the proceedings and to accept the conclusions. We have already made the point that the UN procedure for dealing with complaints would be very much strengthened if non-governmental participation were more generally used there. The fact, however, is that procedures of an exceptional nature, such as those just described, exist as a sort of last resort in cases in which the regular supervisory machinery is inadequate and a more thorough examination is called for.

Where the ILO investigations do link up closely with the UN procedures is in those inquiries undertaken by a UN–ILO *ad hoc* Committee on Forced Labour, as well as an ILO Committee on Forced Labour which existed between 1951 and 1959. These inquiries helped to bring about radical changes of policy and practice in a large number of countries, and led to the adoption of the Abolition of Forced Labour Convention in 1957. The more informal UN Committee on Slavery, set up subsequently to this, was explained in Chapter 1.

Freedom from forced labour has, in fact, been dealt with in two separate ILO Conventions. The Forced Labour Convention, 1930 (No. 29) provided for the progressive abolition of forced labour in all its forms. Pending this abolition, its use for public purposes, only as an exceptional measure, was subject to conditions set out in detail in the Convention. Bearing in mind its date, the 1930 Convention approached forced labour from the point of view of practices then current in colonial territories. The abolition of such systems was one of the main objectives of the 1957 Abolition of Forced Labour Convention (No. 105) which calls for the immediate and complete abolition of forced or compulsory labour for political purposes, and for using labour for economic development or labour discipline, or as a punishment for strike action or as a means of racial, social, national or religious discrimination.

Freedom of Association

The ILO attaches primary importance to those human rights designed to improve the conditions of workers. These fundamental rights are set out in the Conventions and Recommendations on Freedom of Association and Freedom from Discrimination, in addition to Freedom from Forced Labour mentioned above.

These Conventions on basic human rights are not only among the most important, but they are also those which have been ratified by the largest number of countries. Thus, by March 1979, the two Freedom of Association Conventions (Nos. 87 and 98) had been ratified by 91 and 107 countries respectively, and the two Conventions on the abolition of forced labour (Nos. 29 and 105) had been ratified by 119 and 103 countries respectively. The Convention on Freedom from Discrimination in Employment (No. 111), which had been ratified by 96 countries, is worthy of comment. In 1958 the Conference adopted this Convention and Recommendation on discrimination in employment, referring to discrimination on grounds of race, sex, religion, social origin, or political opinion and so on. They define discriminatory laws or acts as 'any distinction, exclusion or preference . . . which has the effect of nullifying or impairing equality of treatment', and cover all sectors of employment and occupation, both public and private. They extend to vocational training and access to employment in general as well as to particular occupations. Methods for combating discrimination range from direct intervention through legislation to educational activities, and include action both by the State and by employers' and workers' organisations.

Freedom of association, to which we now turn, occupies a unique place among the basic human rights protected by ILO law-making procedures. This is because progress towards social justice depends on the workers being able to give expression to their needs and aspirations. It strengthens their position in collective bargaining by establishing a 'balance' in the strength of the parties and also by providing a counter-weight to the power of the State, thus enabling labour to participate in carrying out economic and social policies.

Freedom of association is a principle that we have seen running through the whole ILO system, based as it is on co-operation between workers, employers and governments. It stands in the preamble to the ILO Constitution of 1919, was reaffirmed in the Declaration of Philadelphia, and is embodied in a number of texts adopted by the Conference.

Several of these Conventions (such as Nos. 87 and 98) have been reinforced by other instruments concerning trade union rights and labour-management relations.[2] We can instance the Consultation (Industrial and National Levels) Recommendation of 1960 (No. 113), which urges measures to promote co-operation between public authorities and employers' and workers' organisations, with a view to improving

conditions of work and raising standards of living. There is also the
1971 Convention (No. 135) and a Recommendation (No. 143) concerning the protection afforded to the workers' representatives in order
to support them in their trade union activities in the undertaking or
because of their union membership. These and similar Conventions
commit the ratifying States to facilitate the development of strong and
independent organisations of workers.

Moreover, a resolution concerning trade union rights and their
relation to civil liberties was adopted by the Conference in 1970. This
resolution lists the civil liberties that are essential for the normal exercise of trade union rights, namely the right to freedom and security of
person and freedom from arbitrary arrest and detention; freedom of
opinion and expression; freedom of assembly; the right to a fair trial
by an independent and impartial tribunal; and the right to protection
of trade union property. This book does not aim to be an assessment
or political evaluation of trade unionism in the present context of
national or world affairs, but its emphasis must always be on the rights
of the *individual* worker and on the national and international machinery
which has been devised to assure and enhance them.

Special Procedures

Against this legal background we can now consider those special procedures for the examination of complaints regarding infringements of
trade union rights. As we have already pointed out, these special procedures supplement but are not substitutes for either of the regular supervisory procedures described above. The procedures we now examine
can be brought into play *against governments*, even if they have not
ratified the Freedom of Association Conventions, membership of the
ILO being itself conditional upon the formal acceptance of the obligations of the ILO Constitution, which sets down the principles all members are obligated to uphold.

In fact, it should be pointed out that the ILO's special machinery
was established on the basis of a formal agreement between the ILO
and the Economic and Social Council (ECOSOC). The machinery established as a result of the ILO-UN agreement comprises two bodies: a
Fact-Finding and Conciliation Commission and the Governing Body
Committee on Freedom of Association. The Fact-Finding and Conciliation Commission on Freedom of Association (established in 1950) is
comprised of highly qualified, independent persons appointed by the
ILO Governing Body for examining complaints concerning alleged
infringements of trade union rights. The Commission generally works

in panels composed of three members. It is essentially a fact-finding body, but also discusses the problems referred to it for investigation with the government concerned with a view to securing an agreed solution. Only a complaint submitted by a government or by an employers' or workers' organisation is receivable. But the applicant organisation must be either a national one with a direct interest in the subject matter, an international one in consultative status with the ILO, or some other international employers' or workers' organisation, if the allegations directly affect its affiliated organisations.

Special arrangements have been agreed upon between ECOSOC and the ILO Governing Body concerning allegations received by the United Nations regarding infringements of trade union rights. If complaints against ILO member States are received by the United Nations, they are forwarded by ECOSOC to the ILO, and the Governing Body then considers their referral to the Commission. If the United Nations or the ILO receives a complaint against a country that is a member of the United Nations, but not a member of the ILO, it is for ECOSOC to decide what action to take in the matter. Such a case occurred in 1978 when Costa Rica was the subject of a serious complaint brought against the United States, not then a member of ILO.

However, no case can be submitted to the Commission for investigation unless the government concerned has agreed. The necessity of obtaining the consent of the government concerned has often blocked this procedure, and the first governments which were approached refused to give their consent. But in 1964 the first case was brought before the Commission, with the agreement of Japan. A further three cases have been examined by the Commission, namely, Greece (1965-6), Lesotho (1973-5) and Chile (1974-5). The case of Chile is taken up in our next chapter.

The Governing Body Committee on Freedom of Association was set up by the Governing Body in 1951. The initial stage was merely to carry out a preliminary examination with a view to determining whether a complaint was sufficiently well founded to warrant submission to the Commission. However, because it was difficult to bring cases before the Commission, as noted above, the Committee developed into a body that examines the substance of the cases and submits its findings to the Governing Body. It consists of nine members appointed by the Governing Body — three each from government, workers' and employers' members — and it meets in Geneva three times a year. The functions of the Committee are of a quasi-judicial nature and its procedure conforms to the basic principles of proceedings in a court of law.

Complaints must be submitted either by workers' or employers' organisations or by governments. When a complaint is received it is communicated to the Government for its observations, while the complainant organisation is given a specified period to supply further information, which is also communicated to the Government. The Committee may decide that the substance of a government's reply should be communicated to the complainants for comments, to which the Government will be given the opportunity to reply in turn. If certain governments fail to reply, the Committee submits a report on the case and wider publicity is then given to the original allegations; yet it is seldom necessary to have recourse to such action.

On the basis of the evidence submitted the Committee examines the arguments of the parties and formulates its conclusions. This may consist in the dismissal of a complaint, in its entirety or in part, or of a statement to the effect that a case of infringement has been made out. In this case it draws the attention of the government concerned to the ILO standards that have been infringed, and recommends the steps that should be taken to remedy the situation. In particularly urgent or serious cases the Director-General may, with the approval of the Chairman of the Committee, request the government concerned to allow a representative to carry out an inquiry on the spot with a view to drawing up a report on the facts, on which the Committee can subsequently base its conclusions. This 'direct contacts' procedure has been successfully used in several cases. If an infringement of trade union rights has thus been established, the government concerned may be asked by the Governing Body to take remedial action and to report back within a specific time on the action taken. Moreover, if the Government has ratified the Freedom of Association Conventions, the matter is referred to the Committee of Experts on the Application of Conventions and Recommendations so that it may be followed up under the regular supervision procedure.

This procedure has now been operating for over a quarter of a century. It has dealt with about 1,000 cases, covering an enormous variety of factual and legal situations, and has pronounced on allegations of infringements of trade union rights in every part of the world. Subjects that have frequently been brought before the Committee are the setting up of organisations and the right to join them, election to and removal from trade union office, non-interference with trade union activities, dissolution or suspension of organisations, acts of anti-union discrimination in employment, the right to collective bargaining, the right to strike, arrests of trade unionists, and the prohibition of trade union meetings and demonstrations.

It is clear from this short summary of ILO machinery that trade union rights and individual civil liberties are closely combined. In fact, the Committee has stressed the importance it attaches to respect for fundamental rights and freedoms in dealing with the complaints that have come before it. It has stated that a genuinely *free and independent trade union movement can develop only under a political regime that guarantees human rights.*

In particular, the Committee has been guided by the basic principles set out in the Universal Declaration of Human Rights. To take just one of these basic liberties, the Committee is often confronted with the arrest of trade unionists. Here the Committee has always considered, in fact insisted, that it falls upon the governments concerned to furnish proof that the arrest had no connection with trade union activities. And when a government has replied that in reality trade union leaders or workers have been arrested for subversive activities, for example, for reasons of internal security or for ordinary crimes, then the Committee has requested the government to provide more precise information concerning the arrests, including the full texts of any judgements. Likewise, in every case, the Committee has called for a prompt and fair trial by an independent and impartial judiciary.

Finally, we can ask: 'To what extent is it possible to measure the results achieved by the Committee on Freedom of Association over the years?' In a number of cases, particularly those connected with a difficult political situation, the results have been disappointing, as in the cases cited in Chapter 6, where both trade union and civil rights have continued to be violated, regardless of recommendations made by the Committee. In a great many cases, however, tangible results have been achieved. In such instances, legislation criticised by the Committee has been repealed or amended, practices incompatible with freedom of association have been discontinued, and situations giving rise to complaints have been remedied. In other cases, imprisoned trade union leaders have been released, and in some instances death sentences have been commuted. Moreover, the mere possibility of recourse to a complaints procedure has sometimes led the parties to remedy an existing situation in order to avoid having it investigated at the international level. There may also be cases in which a government refrains from taking measures affecting freedom of association because the Committee might be asked to intervene. Doubtless, in looking back over these 25 years, the greatest achievement of the ILO procedure lies in its gaining universal recognition for the validity of the principles of freedom

of association and in establishing international accountability by governments for their trade union policies.

ILO Under Attack

Before leaving the subject of complaints, however, it must be noted that
the whole ILO half-century edifice was subjected to great strain in the
late 1970s by reason of a systematic opposition coming from certain
quarters, whose own record in ratifying ILO Conventions has been
lamentably deficient. This opposition unfortunately has not been spelled
out in terms indicting the Organisation for specific failures to carry out
its primary protective functions, but rather the assault on the ILO's
worth and integrity has been of the oblique twilight variety. This has
made it more difficult for the ILO's champions to counter charges
expressed in abstract terms, quite apart from the fact that United
Nations institutions do not possess the advantage of a 'right of reply'
against the spokesmen of sovereign states who are naturally immune,
if not indifferent, to outside correction.

These fair-weather critics alleged that the ILO had shown a 'selective
concern' regarding the application of its basic human rights Conventions. In other words, that it ignored violations of human rights in some
parts of the world, limiting its criticisms of such violations to other
parts. In so doing, the Organisation was guilty of applying a so-called
'double standard'. The most damaging (and, in the view of this author,
the unfairest) example was contained in a letter, received in the ILO
on 6 November 1975, constituting a notice of intention of the United
States to withdraw from membership. It was alleged by the then
Secretary of State Henry A. Kissinger that, *inter alia*, the International
Labour Conference 'for some years now has shown an appallingly selective concern in the application of the ILO's basic conventions on freedom of association and forced labour', and he added: 'It pursues the
violation of human rights in some member States. It grants immunity
from such citations to others.'

In order to assess fairly the justification, if any, of allegations of
such broad import, two preconditions have to be met. First, it is necessary to know what *are* the constitutional and other procedures employed
by the ILO in supervising the implementation of ILO Conventions
dealing with basic human rights. Secondly, it is necessary to know the
facts concerning the manner in which these procedures have functioned
in practice, especially in relation to the United States allegations. But
since the first requirement has already been spelled out in detail in the
foregoing pages, it is only necessary in the rest of this chapter to deal

with the second.

There is no question of the seriousness of the ultimate withdrawal of the United States in 1977. It is the only major country to have done so – it places the great United States alongside South Africa, Albania, and Lesotho! Not merely was the ILO partially crippled in its current activities by the dead loss of a quarter of its budget income, but, more importantly, the whole delicate edifice of 'give-and-take', on which the present international order is based, is jeopardised when one powerful state seeks to impose its own interpretation of internationally accepted policies on the world community in the belief that what it conceives to be good for its own domestic interests is good for the world at large.

A challenge of this magnitude cannot be passed over in silence, directed as it is at the moral and constitutional roots of what is undoubtedly the world's leading institution of human rights protection. Since a number of 'small' countries have been brought under serious indictment in this book, it is just and proper that the conduct of the earth's most powerful democracy should be seen and judged in the same context. Not that the United States is itself immune from allegations of human rights violations similar to those of lesser powers. For example, in 1978, a complaint against the United States concerning the torture and death of a Puerto Rican trade union leader was referred to ECOSOC under a routine procedure by the Governing Body of the International Labour Organisation, and the US Government consented to have ECOSOC decide whether the complaint was suitable for investigation by the ILO Fact-Finding and Conciliation Commission on Freedom of Association. This complaint alleged 'serious infringements of trade union freedoms and human rights in Puerto Rico' and it had been sent to the ILO Director-General by the World Federation of Trade Unions. The communication stated that on 11 October 1977 the American police arrested 'two active militant trade union leaders of the TMT shipping company' and that later one leader 'was found dead, his body having been severely tortured'; this case is at present proceeding. But, at this point, our concern is with the validity of the United States' own complaints against the ILO.[3]

One thing is clear: some elements in the United States have long been antagonistic to the purposes and growth of international institutions that have obviously slipped beyond their influence or control. To be understood in its longer term effects this latest 'pull-out', which has brought such distress to the ILO, has to be seen in relation to earlier episodes of unabashed 'politicisation' of the UN's organs and agencies committed by the United States itself.

The earlier financial domination of the UN by the United States (which paid 40 per cent of the budgeted costs until 1960, but then reduced this to 25 per cent) led, it was once said, to 'the heaping on it of presents to reward UN obedience'. But at the 'merest suggestion of UN recalcitrance', the threat appeared in various forms to 'send the Organization to bed without its dinner'. To review some recent examples of this picturesque but not too far-fetched analogy, the World Bank President Robert McNamara and the Bank constantly come under vehement attack by American public opinion, which treats the Bank as a branch of US aid administration and reproaches it for having staff members who are better paid than Americans, and for instance, for supporting in developing countries the production of crops which those countries badly need, but which compete with the surplus production of the United States. The Bank is also under fire for refusing to tie loans to a recognition of human rights in borrowing countries.

The UN Educational, Scientific and Cultural Organisation (UNESCO) is frequently under attack, too, both in Europe and in the US, for over-stepping its mandate, particularly in its condemnation of Israel. Both the General Agreement on Tariffs and Trade (GATT) and the International Monetary Fund (IMF) are attacked, the former for its inability to halt the rise of protectionism and the latter for its inability to reduce the extent of the fluctuations of the major currencies.

A remarkable speech by Charles William Maynes, Assistant-Secretary of State for International Organisation Affairs, made before the Board of Directors of the United Nations Association on November 20, 1978, included this admission:

> The Congress of the United States has not simply followed the example of the Soviet Union — as bad as that example is — and refused to pay for a portion of the United Nations budget with which it disagreed. It has gone beyond this by insisting on attaching conditions to the rest of the U.S. contributions — a step no other member state has ever taken. It is potentially the most damaging blow any member state has directed against the United Nations.

Behind all this, the post-War international economic order, which had worked so profitably, thanks to the hegemony (not only military but also monetary) of the US, has not survived the multi-polar world that has since gradually formed. Realisation of these facts has imbued most other countries with a genuine aspiration to rebuild a new world economic and social order which would take account of their common problems. This means more harmonious North-South relations, which are a constant aim in future international policy-making and which have always been a bedrock of ILO principles. So the ILO is already part of the wave of the future, to which the US finds it more and more difficult to adapt.

The earlier years of US-ILO relations were ambivalent too, because McCarthyism introduced a legacy of deliberate persecution of UN personnel, which took place at a time when the United States attitudes seemed to assume that the UN was a minor branch of its own State Department. By the early 1970s this pattern, of course, began to visibly break down, as many more 'small' countries joined. But it was Senator J. William Fulbright, when he was Chairman of the Senate Foreign Relations Committee of the United States, who pointed out: 'Having controlled the United Nations for many years as tightly and as easily as a big-city boss controls his party machine, we had got used to the idea that the United Nations was a place where we could work our will.'

This pattern, unfortunately, has never ceased to hover in the background and darken the uneasy US-ILO relationship. This unease was due not to defects in the ILO principles or to the democratic system as it had emerged from the carefully drafted Philadelphia agreements (see Chapter 2). It was due rather to US *internal* labour politics and especially to the continuing animosity of top US labour leaders towards a world body committed to treat in terms of constitutional equality social systems which these leaders have always regarded with extreme hostility. When David Morse, an American, retired as Director-General, in 1970, Dr Wilfred Jenks succeeded him and appointed a Russian as one of his Assistant Directors. The AFL-CIO was outraged at this step, and the US Senate voted to withhold US membership dues for a time.

To make matters worse, this mounting conflict – which had been expressing itself in many other ways – was heightened when the ILO Conference in 1975, in conformity with all other organs of the UN system, granted observer status to the Palestine Liberation Organisation. Hence, in 1975, the dissatisfaction of the AFL-CIO – with the concurrence of the US national Chamber of Commerce – pressured the Government to threaten that, if certain conditions were not changed, they would withdraw from the ILO two years thereafter.

The four alleged particulars of complaint to be remedied were: (1) an erosion of the ILO tripartite representation, due to the lack of independence in employer and worker delegates from totalitarian countries; (2) a selective concern for human rights in right-wing countries and disregard of human rights abuse in socialist countries; (3) a disregard of due process in the adoption of resolutions condemning member states (that is, Israel) without prior resort to established procedures; and (4) an increasing politicisation of the ILO in dealing with political matters, such as the Arab condemnation of Israel.

It was obvious that these conditions, even if justified, could not have been met within two years. For one thing, the separating of government from employer and worker representation in totalitarian states could not be changed on the demand of a hostile power; and 'politicisation' of this order was already common to the United Nations and a dozen of its Agencies — most of all, to the United States itself! And the two latter 'conditions' were actually matters that had outwitted the UN's political organs ever since the 1967 Arab-Israeli War.

The ILO itself, however, bravely changed its parliamentary procedures to side-step, at least, an Arab-Israeli confrontation; and went even further and reappointed an Israeli representative to its Governing Body — the only UN Agency to do so. But Mr George Meany, the voice of the AFL-CIO, was not converted, still waging his cold war against the Soviet Union. The Carter administration was unwilling to cross him, so left the field of battle.

But had President Carter listened to the urgings of Secretary of State Cyrus Vance, Senator Hubert Humphrey ('the greatest of living Americans', as he himself had said), UN Ambassador Andrew Young and to all the leaders of Europe, who were unanimously against US withdrawal at that time, as well as to the Pope; and consequently held his hand just one year longer (as was feasible under the ILO constitution), the acute domestic pressure then being exerted upon him -- especially by the pro-Zionist and violently anti-Communist George Meany — might well have been relaxed. Less than 20 days after President Carter's decision on 1 November, President Sadat's heroic confrontation with the Israeli diehards in the lion's lair would have deflated one of Carter's toughest unsolved problems — that is, how to get Israelis and Arabs to sit down together. Viewed in that light, the United States defection was not an act of considered statesmanship at all, but an accident, an abject capitulation to highly emotional domestic wrangles. But the evil had been done, and was too difficult to undo.

Since the US had contributed approximately a quarter of the ILO budget, as stated above, its withdrawal severely injured its immediate on-going work, jeopardising current programmes on freedom of association and the forced labour conventions outlined earlier in this chapter. But the resilience of the Organisation to recover from this financial blow was ready proof that even the most powerful members cannot defy the 'civilised opinion of mankind' with impunity.

In fact, some veteran observers soon noted that the greater loser in the long run was the United States itself. At the time, the Director-General himself, Francis Blanchard, told a press conference: 'There is an enormous disproportion between the United States decision to withdraw and the reasons given by Washington for the move.' Some UN senior officials and long experienced diplomats more bluntly described the US walkout as 'blackmail'. Secretary-General Kurt Waldheim was particularly outspoken in saying: 'The United States withdrawal is a retrogressive step from the principle of collective responsibility.'

The question that remains is: has this latest US political gambit permanently incapacitated the world-wide standard-setting and supervisory functions that we have so strongly endorsed in this book? The answer certainly is 'NO', and for several definite reasons:

(1) Nearly 60 years of coping with international crises – including the Second World War itself – have seen the Organisation emerge from every test with greater confidence, usefulness and stability.

(2) The emphasis throughout its long history has been not on the sovereign state, but on the sovereign *individual* – that is why the tripartite character of the Organisation can face up to the varying ideological prejudices of national governments.

(3) The ILO is no longer standing alone as the world champion of workers' rights; its allies grow with its achievements.

(4) The proven flexibility of the Organisation, especially in meeting human needs, for example, in world employment policy and in assistance to developing countries, opens a far more promising future programme than any single nation could achieve acting by itself.

United States leaders must obviously think again.

Notes

1. For the ILO Missions to Israel, see Chapter 6.
2. For the text of these major Conventions (Nos. 87 and 98) see Appendix B.
3. The validity of the 'politicisation' charges will be taken further in the next chapter, dealing with case studies from both East and West.

6 NINE CASE STUDIES

As stated in the Introduction, no attempt has been made — or would be possible in so limited a space — to compare or contrast this brief selection of case studies with each other or to set them within the relative national contexts or historical situations. No one really knows how many more equally serious or potentially dangerous cases could be added to this chapter, which is of necessity confined to some nine countries. And these have been arranged in simple alphabetical order so as to avoid any semblance of political or moral categorisation.

Passing reference has been made in the preceding chapters to a number of other cases, not specifically included now out of context; but it will be observed that those featured here — out of some two score equally notorious cases that might well have been included — are not confined to any particular part of the world or any particular 'social system'. Yet, these nine examples certainly reflect a common pattern, different though the circumstances may be. There is a military control or a *junta* dictatorship; there is discrimination against sectors of the population; there is always long-term or short-term imprisonment or detention; there is invariably some form of torture or humiliation; and, of course, gross violation of fundamental human rights and freedoms.

Chile

Coming alphabetically first in our short list, it also happens that the sheer bulk of the written and verbal evidence contained in both United Nations and ILO dossiers concerning human rights violations in Chile, since the *junta* took over in September 1973, sets a world record of horror and shame. The latest UN document, summarising events up to February 1979, consists of some 200 closely printed pages, entitled:

> *Study of Reported Violations of Human Rights in Chile, With Particular Reference to Torture and Other Cruel, Inhuman or Degrading Treatment or Punishment*

> Report of the *Ad Hoc* Working Group established under resolution 8 (XXXI) of the Commission on Human Rights to inquire into the situation of human rights in Chile[1]

From these, some 20 pages only relate to our special topic of workers' rights. These concern particularly Freedom of Association and the right of assembly by trade unions. As an instance of this we can briefly review the *junta*'s restrictions resulting in the labour conflict at the copper-mining town of Chuquicamata, which took the form of a so-called 'lunch-box campaign'. The workers at the state-owned copper-mining enterprise called Codelco boycotted the company canteens for a period in protest against the failure to give due consideration to long outstanding wage claims. The declaration of a state of siege in the province where the Chuquicamata mines are situated provided — among other restrictions — for the following:

1. The holding of all meetings, assemblies, demonstrations and gatherings of any kind in the province are hereby prohibited. The Commander of the Zone under State of Siege may, however, authorize the holding of meetings, assemblies or other activities, subject to the submission to the Garrison Commander, not less than 24 hours beforehand, of a written request indicating reasons.

2. The entry of persons into and the departure of persons from the province shall be controlled by the Chilean police.

3. Social, family and religious gatherings, such as weddings, may be held without prior permission, but persons attending such gatherings must ensure that they do not instigate any act likely to result in a disturbance of the peace.

Because of the declaration of this state of siege, the workers were unable to hold meetings. Visits to the zone were restricted to the point where even the Apostolic Administrator of the Prefecture was denied entry, on the orders of the Commander of the Zone, who stated on 18 September 1978: 'Your planned visit is strictly prohibited. For reasons of military security, the movement of vehicles into and out of that area is suspended until further notice.'

Later, about 70 workers charged with using the conflict for political purposes, were arrested under the powers conferred by the state of siege. The majority of them were mineworkers, but there were also residents of the province who had been politically active in parties opposed to the government. Three of them were held under house arrest, but the majority were taken to remote areas, which had harsh climates that adversely affected the health of these detainees. After about a month, the detainees were released, for lack of evidence. A number stated that their health had suffered from their prolonged isolation in the remote areas.

The right of assembly and freedom of expression were likewise subjected to severe restrictions under a proclamation issued by the Commander of the Zone under State of Siege on 7 September 1978, which stated, *inter alia*: 'I warn any person who is thinking of acting with the obvious intent of disrupting public order, that he will be subjected to the full force of the law, and that he cannot expect the slightest leniency, since he will be acting against all Chileans and against his own country.' And to this he added:

Organizations, clubs, associations and other groups wishing to hold meetings of any kind must request the appropriate authorization 48 hours beforehand at the Headquarters of the Military Garrison or at the Office of the Provincial Governor, it being clearly understood that the submission of a request does not mean that authorization has been granted.

Under this 'controlled freedom' of the state of emergency, the normal media are prevented from disseminating information constituting 'anti-patriotic propaganda'. The *junta* expect only 'responsible and correct attitudes by the provincial media'. Moreover, 'it must be clearly understood that any person making statements deliberately or maliciously shall render himself liable to penalties to be determined by the Commander of the Zone'. The proclamation that any person who is thinking of acting with intent to disrupt public order will be subjected to the full force of the law, implies that the authorities are empowered to carry out repressive measures on the basis of the opinions of individuals. In fact, the threat contained in this proclamation was carried out in the cases of several persons who were arrested and never brought to trial, despite the serious charges made against them in official statements.

The UN Group reported that the restrictions on the rights of assembly and freedom of expression imposed in the Zone are directly related to the attitude of the *junta* towards labour problems. Sergio de Castro, Minister of Finance, for example, said that talks between the enterprise and the workers 'must be conducted in an atmosphere totally free of any pressure'; but the Vice-President for Marketing of Codelco, Colonel Gaston Fernandez, stated quite clearly: 'If wage negotiations are to take place, we are not prepared to accept pressure'. Such statements show quite clearly that the purpose of the described measures was to prevent the mineworkers from exerting any pressure with a view to securing progress in the negotiations towards meeting their repeated claims. Hence, the workers had to confine themselves to drawing attention to their problems, without adopting positions that might have entailed drastic measures. The following statement sheds some light on the leaders' invidious position:

> In view of the lack of response to the requests which we have made over the past two years and which were reiterated in a document delivered over a month ago to the government authorities and to Codelco, we find ourselves in the painful position of having to return to Chuquicamata with a feeling of frustration and disillusion in our hearts, caused by the indignation that would be felt by anyone who considers himself to have been cheated when, in exercising his right to call on the authorities to solve his economic problems, he receives the moral slap in the face of red tape or is met with the deafness of insensitivity.

Subsequently, some improvements were granted to the workers, according to the UN investigations stretching over five years. Of those who had been arrested, however, not all were able to keep their jobs. Codelco called for the resignations of 53 of the 72 persons arrested for alleged 'political' reasons. Moreover, those workers were forced to leave the province and were forbidden to return, as long as the state of siege lasted. In commenting on this situation, the UN Group felt compelled to state that

> the restrictions imposed on human rights were disproportionate to the exigencies of the situation prevailing in the Zone . . . A number of the orders and rules put into effect adversely affect freedom of thought and conscience, as has already been pointed out – freedoms which may not be restricted even in situations presenting a genuine threat to the life of the nation.

The Group also recorded that these restrictions imposed on the right of assembly and freedom of expression 'place insurmountable obstacles in the way of workers' participation in the decision-making process in matters of direct concern to them'.

In October 1978 the Minister of the Interior announced a number of measures that were being taken by the government in the labour field. These included the promulgation of a decree-law giving special powers to the Minister empowering him to recommend to the Head of State the dismissal of any official who 'impedes the exercise of the rights of the public, and to eliminate or simplify, in the various departments, unnecessarily bureaucratic procedures that are incompatible with a modern society . . .' In the next few days the Government made known its plan to create 'a new institutional framework for trade unions, which would contrast with the politicization and divisiveness trade unionism had suffered from in the past, when it had been made an instrument of party politics'.

A large number of decree-laws were to implement these principles. For example, a Decree-Law (No. 2,345) stated specifically that the Minister of the Interior shall not be obstructed 'by reason of the existence of legal rights or tenure of any kind, and shall not be subject to the Administrative Statute or to other similar organic provisions'. If the officials in charge of the public sector are thus deprived of their union rights, by the repeal of the provisions affording them the necessary protection, then it will be possible for workers' representatives to be dismissed by a simple decision of the Executive Power. Not only are representatives therefore deprived of protection from action by the authorities, but all state workers will be without adequate representation of their interests.

Again, another provision of the same Decree-Law constituted a warning to all employees of the Administration and of state enterprises, that their right to work will henceforth be afforded no legal protection of any kind. Its stated aim was

> to achieve efficiency in the functioning of the services of the State administration in all its aspects; in other words, the expeditious execution of the provisions which govern State activity, consideration and concern for the users of the services, and effective management of the services .

The scope of the powers conferred on the Executive Power to dismiss 'any official of the State administration, regardless of the capacity in which he works' would not be limited by any of the existing rules that have hitherto governed the labour rights of state employees.

Many detailed and documented reports were given in previous years by the aforementioned UN Group on the removal of trade union leaders and their replacement by other persons who supported the Government, as well as the dissolution of their unions and subsequent replacement by pro-government unions. In addition, the Government ordered the confiscation of all their assets, which were transferred to the state. The trade-union organisations concerned in this nation-wide havoc comprised 550 unions with membership of 400,000 workers, according to the leaders of the dissolved unions.

How, then, does this devastation of workers' rights square with the ILO Code? The protection of workers' organisations by the administrative authorities of the state is covered by such international rules for the protection of trade union rights as in article 4 of ILO Convention No. 87 of 1948, where it is stated that: 'Workers' and employers' organizations shall not be liable to be dissolved or suspended by administrative authority'.

In fact, as a result of the complaint presented by the dissolved trade union organisations, the ILO Committee on Freedom of Association reported to the Governing Body in November 1978 as follows:

> Whatever the reasons invoked by the Government in the legislative decree dissolving these organisations, the Committee must point out that the procedure followed in these cases for the dissolution of these organisations is not compatible with the principle that workers' organisations should not be dissolved by administrative authority. The measures taken are of a particularly serious nature since affiliated organisations are also affected under the legislative decree, and their assets transferred to the State (article 4 of the decree). . .

It should be explained that Chile had not ratified the Freedom of Association and Protection of the Right to Organise Convention 1948 (No. 87), which, accordingly, has no binding effect for that country. However, by its membership of the International Labour Organisation, Chile is bound to respect a certain number of rules which have been established for the common good of the peoples of the twentieth century. Chile cannot contract out of the world, at the whim of its military dictatorship. Freedom of association has become a customary rule above the Conventions. As the Committee on Freedom of Association of the Governing Body indicated in a report approved by the latter as long ago as March 1952: 'The function of the International Labour Organisation in regard to trade union rights is to contribute to the effectiveness of the general principle of freedom of association as one of the primary safeguards of peace and social justice'. The Committee further indicated that it would not hesitate to discuss in an international forum cases which

are of such a character as to affect substantially the aims and purposes of the ILO as set forth in the Constitution, the Declaration of
Philadelphia, and the Conventions concerning freedom of association.

The government of Chile agreed to its case being referred to the
Fact-Finding and Conciliation Commission on Freedom of Association (see Chapter 5) and facilitated its visit to Chile in 1974. Having
defined the legal framework in which the Commission carried out its
task, the Commission formulated its recommendations, pointing out
that the events which occurred on 11 September 1973 brought about
far-reaching changes in Chile and a complete reversal of the situation
which prevailed in the country before that date. 'It is obvious that the
country was, and still is, deeply divided,' reported the Commission. 'It
is not, however, the task of the Commission to express an opinion on
the causes which led to these events, nor upon the appropriateness of
the decision to effect these changes. These are highly controversial
political issues which are outside its competence.'[2]

In terms, then, of a non-political appraisal, the ILO on-the-spot
investigation showed that both the Government and the witnesses on
its behalf, as well as the many persons interviewed in Chile, insisted
on the need to bear in mind the situation which existed in the country
immediately prior to the above date, and which was said to have ac-
counted for the change of regime. But the Commission insisted that,
whatever this situation may have been, its terms of reference were to
investigate the various allegations of infringement of freedom of association and civil rights, as they affected the exercise of trade union
rights, since the change of regime. Moreover, the Commission rightly
emphasised that:

> The events in Chile have had a profound impact upon public
> opinion, and upon all trends of thought in the international trade
> union movement, irrespective of their political leanings or ideo-
> logies. The complaints presented to the ILO contain grave accus-
> ations not only of infringement of trade union rights but also, and
> in particular, of infringement of basic human rights pertaining to
> the lives, personal safety and freedom of many trade unionists.

It was clear to the Commission that the real intention behind the
change of regime was to bring about a drastic change in the situation
as it had developed under the Popular Unity Government. The action
of the new government could not fail, therefore, to have a profound
impact upon the trade union movement, a substantial proportion of

whose leaders were members of Popular Unity parties. In its conclusion the report stated:

> The links then existing between trade union officials and political parties are a fact which is not denied by anyone, and moreover such links were long-standing in Chile and were reflected in union election results.

And further,

> The Commission has analysed the various items of evidence at its disposal, bearing in mind also the large number of trade union officials and organisations affected by measures taken by authorities at different levels. It is clear from all this evidence, viewed as a whole, that one of the aims of the Government has been to eliminate or prevent any large-scale opposition to its policy on the part of trade unions or of large numbers of their leaders.

Since it is not feasible to devote more space to this outstanding example of an ILO investigation, we can draw attention to the opening pages (reproduced here as Appendix D) of a list of names of trade union leaders killed or executed, which was appended to the Commission's report.

To conclude the present section, however, we can perhaps revert to the United Nations Working Group study, which fully confirmed the ILO Commission's findings and which was adopted by the UN Commission on Human Rights in March 1978, when Dr Félix Ermacora of Austria, a member of the Group, recalled that the Government of Chile had been slowly yielding to world-wide pressure and had demonstrated 'a kind of co-operation' with the United Nations. Unwarranted arrests, tortures and other gross violations of human rights, he said, had diminished in numbers. The state of siege had been replaced by the state of emergency, and the notorious police operation, DINA, was now replaced. At the same time, it was difficult for the exiled Chileans to return to their country. Moreover, without the efforts of the church, the economic situation of the broad masses would have been even worse, because trade unions were not able to meet their needs and aspirations.

It was at this meeting of the Human Rights Commission that further evidence was presented on the fate of the '200 disappeared persons'. One of the witnesses, Señora Maureira Muñoz, told the Commission that her father and four brothers had been arrested in 1973, and she had been unable to learn where they were. The police had said they had been transferred to the National Stadium, and would be interrogated as 'terrorist elements'. After that she and her mother had not received any further information about the fates of her father and brothers. Later, the authorities even denied that her father and brothers had been arrested. But recently, she said, the mutilated bodies of her father and her four brothers had been found in a mining shaft and were identified by her sister with the help of a dentist. In her small village of not more than 2,000 inhabitants near Santiago, there were at least six other families confronted with the same fate. This fact reflected the magnitude of the problem of disappeared persons in Chile.

After considering the Group's report, the 1978 UN General Assembly, meeting in New York, called once more upon the Chilean authorities 'to restore and safeguard, without delay, basic human rights and fundamental freedoms'. It urged the Chilean authorities, *inter alia:*

(a) To cease the state of emergency, under which continued violations of human rights and fundamental freedoms are permitted;[3]

(b) To restore the democratic institutions and constitutional safeguards formerly enjoyed by the Chilean people;

(c) To ensure an immediate end to torture and other forms of inhuman or degrading treatment, and to prosecute and punish those responsible for such practices;

(d) To cease arbitrary arrest and detention and to release immediately those who are imprisoned for political reasons;

(e) To restore fully the right of habeas corpus;

(f) To restore Chilean nationality to those who have been deprived of it for political reasons;

(g) To guarantee the standards of labour protection called for by international instruments and fully restore previously established trade union rights;

(h) To fully guarantee freedom of expression;

(i) To take urgent and effective measures in response to the profound international concern at the fate of persons reported to have disappeared for political reasons, and in particular to investigate and clarify the fate of these persons.

Czechoslovakia

What became known in 1978 as the 'Charter 77' Manifesto on Human

Rights Movement has grown from 300 signatures at the beginning of
that year to at least 1,000 despite tough measures against it by Czechoslovak authorities. It soon brought a sharp decision by the ILO Governing Body in accordance with the procedure laid down for cases in which
a government's reply 'is not deemed to be satisfactory'.

The complaint against Czechoslovakia, first lodged by the International Confederation of Free Trade Unions (ICFTU) in January
1977, alleged that the Government had failed to observe the Discrimination (Employment and Occupation) Convention which it had ratified
in 1964. In its reply the Government stated that the complaint was
'wholly unfounded'. So, the case was examined for over a year by the
main government – employer – worker Committee appointed by the
Governing Body in accordance with ILO's machinery for monitoring
the observance by states of international labour standards. As a result
of this careful examination, the Governing Body decided, by a vote of
38 in favour, 4 against and 9 abstentions, that the government's reply
was not satisfactory and that the whole dossier of its investigation
should be published. The decision to publicise the dossier was considered the strongest action yet taken by the ILO against an East
European country. At the end of this world-wide exposure, which
enabled everyone to see the facts, the playwright Vaclav Havel, who
has been placed under house arrest, said; 'The fact that the Charter
survives is already an achievement'.[4]

The Manifesto asked for a dialogue with Czechoslovak Communist
authorities on extending human rights in Czechoslovakia, and on past
human rights violations. The regime reacted at once with harsh measures, including the arrest of Mr Havel, who was one of several spokesmen for the movement at the time.

Professor Jiri Hajek, another of the founders of the Charter 77 group,
had submitted details of 46 cases of alleged persecution, including 19
who were dismissed for having signed Charter 77. He contended that
'most who have lost their jobs cannot find other work. The State is
the only employer, and the only institution directing the operations of
justice'. But, the Czech Government said that equality of opportunity
and freedom of speech were guaranteed by the Czech Constitution, and
that dismissal without notice is prohibited by the 1975 Labour Code,
except where 'the security of the State (Section 53), or labour discipline is threatened'.

Concluding its itemised complaint against the Czech Government,
ICFTU stated:

Experience of the proceedings in the law courts hearing these labour disputes proves that the courts identify themselves with the above-mentioned punitive action. It often happens that investigation of evidence and of the legality of dismissals is avoided, and the validity of dismissal accepted, merely by reference to the statement drawn up by the Chief State Counsel on the subject of the Charter. Charter 77 is not even read out to the court and does not form part of the examining magistrate's file. Accordingly, the court cannot see whether employers' arguments are sound, and it does not even try to do so. Examples of such judgments are the verdicts of the Court of District 1 of Prague in the case of Zdenek Mlynar (45), Zd. Jicinsky (46) and Jiri Pallas (47).

The judges would not even dare to look for real causes as legal standards require them to, for they know very well what would happen to them if they decided in favour of the plaintiffs. This would amount to the discovery that in fact Charter 77 is not an attack upon the safety of the State and that signing it is not a serious infringement of work discipline; and that accordingly the dismissals are invalid.[5]

The importance of this case, which the London *Times* (19 June 1978) described as 'A Test Case for the ILO', cannot be denied, since publicity in the long run is a powerful weapon against governments who direct much of their foreign relations to saving face. For, as *The Times* pointed out, the case against the Czech Government was

> overwhelming, as the letters and other documents attached to the Committee's report show. The letters from employers to employees, the texts of court decisions, the letter from the official trade union movement, all make the same point: that those concerned were being dismissed for the single offence of signing Charter 77. Since this is a clear violation of the ILO's Convention 111, which says that no one may lose his job because of his political beliefs, the evidence submitted to the ILO spoke for itself.

It may well be that the wheels of a 150-member organisation, such as the ILO, turn slowly, and it will obviously be some time before this affair is concluded. What has happened thus far is that the relevant Committee has found the allegations against Czechoslovakia well documented, and dismissed the Czechoslovak defence as too general and evasive. In view of the unsatisfactory reply from the Czech Government, the case now goes back to the Committee of Experts and to the International Labour Conference Committee to pursue whatever steps they may decide to take.

Equatorial Guinea

When, upon independence in 1968, the new President Mr Macias Nguema assumed dictatorial power, he appointed himself President for life, as well as Major-General of the Armed Forces, Grand Maestro of Popular Education, Science and Traditional Culture, and President of the Unique National Workers' Party; and he has since assumed the portfolios of Defence, Foreign Affairs and Trade. He is probably the only modern African leader to have made use of primitive tribal beliefs and cults for political ends.

According to a report of the International Commission of Jurists:

> He is utterly ruthless in liquidating his political opponents. Countless members of the pre-independence intelligentsia have disappeared, been tortured, executed without trial or are now in exile. More than two-thirds of the members of the independence Assembly have disappeared and ten of the twelve independence Cabinet members are now dead.[6]

Information available during the past four years has demonstrated that little has been improved for the citizens of this unfortunate nation. Their lives are governed by economic dislocation, resulting in a disastrous decline in production, massive unemployment and meagre diets. Arbitrary and tyrannical enforcement of authority, frequently marked by torture and extra-judicial execution, is the norm. These are the principal factors which have lead to an exodus of tens of thousands, of the nation's population of something over 400,000, into the neighbouring countries of Africa and to Europe.

The International Commission of Jurists has interviewed refugees from Equatorial Guinea in the preparation of a communication describing the violations of human rights in their country, which was submitted to the UN Secretary-General under ECOSOC Resolution 1503, that calls on the UN Commission on Human Rights to examine gross and well attested violations of human rights. In March 1979, the Commission agreed to make a thorough study of what is going on in Equatorial Guinea, and it was, in fact, singled out as one of nine countries on which the Commission had decided to take action under that Resolution.

Non-governmental organisations have helped to keep this issue before public opinion. Amnesty International recently forwarded a communication tò the Chairman of the Organisation of African Unity detailing a 'succession of arbitrary arrests, death from torture and summary execution'. The European Economic Community recently determined that no economic aid to Equatorial Guinea would be forthcoming in the light of its human rights record. And President Carter promised prominent exiles that the US Government would bear in mind the human rights situation in the regime in any further dealings with that country.

Meantime, Presidential decrees forbid many actions by individuals which are internationally recognised rights, and they have made many offences punishable by death. Individuals can be detained for giving aid to missionaries, failing to attend national manifestations of praise and joy, or merely for being 'descontento'. Such wide sweeping prohibitions leave nearly everyone subject to 'criminal' proceedings, for there is a complete breakdown of judicial process. Moreover, the militia is formed by youth from the *Juventud en marcha con Macias* (Youth on the March with Macias), and the Security Chief encourages youngsters in the village to inform on anybody: family, neighbours and others.

Prisoners in solitary confinement are held in cells 160 cm by 60 cm, with no windows, no light and scant ventilation. Prisoners are kept naked, or given only underpants, and must stand all day without touching the walls. They are let out only for interrogations or 'ceremonies' involving degradation and punishment. Recent refugee reports give a glimpse of the more advanced forms of torture used at Blackbirch prison: *El Balanceo*; the prisoner is hung upside down from tied or shackled feet, then swung around and beaten, *La Colgadura*; the same, except that the prisoner is hoisted by a rope tied to manacles around his wrists, *Las Tablillas*; planks of wood are pressed against the sides of the calf, ankle and the under part of the foot and progressively tightened by ropes. Many other forms of degrading punishment are meted out, and many prisoners die from the torture. According to reports, many others go insane or become suicidal.

A report of the Anti-Slavery Society in London says:

> The catalogue of death concentrates only on the best-known political leaders and says nothing of the hundreds of men, women and children who were unknown outside their country when they met similar fates. In many cases people have been punished or executed without even a pretence that they were guilty of a crime . . . in some cases whole villages have been destroyed when a member of the comm-

unity was accused of disloyalty to Macias or some such crime.

The dire misery of this satanic system is that, at the time of independence, Equatorial Guinea had one of the highest per capita incomes in Africa and one of the most developed political and economic infrastructures. The economy is now a shambles and the infrastructure, both human and physical, is devastated. Even the Catholic Church which had been the primary source of schools is prohibited from engaging in the education of the citizens of the country. Earlier in 1978, the remaining Spanish priests in Equatorial Guinea were expelled, but not before a ransom for their release had to be paid by the Spanish Government.

Concerning workers' rights, as such, the nation's cocoa plantations traditionally relied on migrant labourers from neighbouring African countries. But, under the Macias regime, life for the workers has steadily worsened. There were reports in 1970 and 1971 that 95 Nigerians were killed in Fernando Po for demanding their arrears in wages. Things became so bad that in 1975 the Nigerian Government evacuated 10,000 nationals by plane and many thousands more by ship. These evacuations left the plantations without workers to harvest the crops. The response to this situation was compulsory labour. In January 1976, the Congress of the Unique National Workers Party (PUNT), the only legal party and one in which membership by all is compulsory, called for a system of compulsory labour. A Presidential decree in March of that year made it mandatory for all citizens over the age of 15 years to render manual labour in government plantations and mines.

In 1977, 25,000 persons, with some 15,000 dependants were 'recruited' under this scheme. These workers are not paid a salary. The sole remuneration for each worker is 20 kg of rice, 4 litres of palm oil, and four kg of fish per month. No account is taken of the number of dependants a worker may have to support, so it is clearly insufficient for even a small family. The workday for such workers is the daylight period, year round. In addition to the strenuous labour, the work conditions include beatings, withholding of food rations, molestation of women of all ages, random brutality and occasional killings. There is no medical care, no freedom to communicate with relatives or freedom to return home. No wonder that, since 'independence', many thousands have fled Equatorial Guinea. Estimates suggest that the refugees have numbered as many as 100,000 or nearly 25 per cent of the population.

Although not specifically concerned with workers' rights, as such, the Commission on Human Rights has had these appalling conditions on its black list for some time and in March 1979 appointed a Special Rapporteur to examine the facts and to give a detailed report to the Commission at its next session.

Indonesia

In 1977, the ILO noted that large numbers of workers and other persons had been detained for periods of ten years or more without having been tried by a court of law. Some 10,000 of these detainees had been installed on the island of Buru, which they were not free to leave and where they had no other choice than to work in a narrow range of jobs provided for in a resettlement programme. The Committee of Experts concluded that the detainees could not be considered to have offered themselves voluntarily for the work in question, and were therefore performing forced labour within the meaning of the Convention, which Indonesia had ratified in 1950. Furthermore, according to allegations made in the ILO Conference Committee in 1974, detainees in other parts of Indonesia had been forced to work on major construction projects. In reply, the government stated, in March 1977, that a number of detainees had been released and gave an undertaking to the Conference Committee that the entire matter would be settled by the end of 1978, by the trial or release of all remaining detainees.

According to the government's later report, it had released a total of 2,500 detainees by the end of 1976 and it intended to return to society 10,000 persons in 1977, another 10,000 during 1978, and the remaining detainees in 1979. The government stated, however, that there were certain problems. First, there must be sufficient employment for the released detainees. For this reason, the government planned to establish resettlement areas in Sumatra, Kalimantan, Sulawesi and other places. Those who came from Java, due to the density of the population, will be transmigrated to other islands. Budgetary requirements for resettlement and transmigration were main reasons for the timetable indicated. Second, the released detainees would have to prove their good citizenship through concrete deeds in an adjustment process which might take time and which required supervision. The ILO Committee took due note of these explanations, but required detailed information on the action taken, including the number of persons tried, the numbers still awaiting trial and the measures taken to ensure that persons who were acquitted or whose sentences did not involve further detention were permitted to recover their free choice of employment.

As the case was still a live issue before the ILO, the Government stated in a report dated 8 March 1978 that on 20 December 1977,

10,000 detainees were simultaneously released from 'rehabilitation centres' all over Indonesia, including 1,500 detainees on Buru Island, and that the number of remaining detainees was 19,791; these were to be released in 1978 and 1979. According to the Government, these releases were to be absolute and unconditional. If, however, living as ordinary free citizens in the community, 'these ex-detainees should later encounter difficulties to obtain jobs, or had family troubles, then the Government is ready to assist them by offering them accommodation and the opportunity towards a decent living in one of the several resettlement projects being established by the Government for this purpose, within the framework of the national transmigration programme'. The government emphasised that these resettlement projects could be taken advantage of by the ex-detainees on a *voluntary basis.*

With regard to detainees whom it was proposed to bring to trial, the government indicated that by the end of 1978 all cases would be settled either through adjudication or through reclassification. The Committee of Experts noted this information with interest, but expressed the hope that the government would supply detailed information on the number of persons tried or still awaiting trial, and the measures taken to ensure that persons who were acquitted or whose sentences did not involve further detention were to be permitted to recover their free choice of employment. So the surveillance by the ILO continues in the light of the full publicity exercised by the Conference and its expert investigatory bodies, as well as through its published reports.[7]

Palestine

In a large number of resolutions, the General Assembly has recognised that the people of Palestine are entitled to 'equal rights and self-determination' in accordance with the Charter of the United Nations, and has confirmed the legality of the Palestinian people's struggle for self-determination. Moreover, in 1975 the Assembly established a Committee on the Exercise of the Inalienable Rights of the Palestinian People, composed of 20 Member States, to recommend action which the Assembly and the Security Council might take to enable the Palestinian people to exercise their rights.

Since 1976, both the Council and the Assembly have considered reports prepared by the Committee. In addition, the Economic and Social Council has considered reports by the Secretary-General on UN assistance to the Palestinian people. And in 1977, the General Assembly reaffirmed that 'a just and lasting peace in the Middle East cannot be

established without the achievement, among other things, of a just
solution of the problem of Palestine on the basis of the attainment of
the inalienable rights of the Palestinian people, including the right of
return and the right to national independence and sovereignty in
Palestine, in accordance with the Charter of the United Nations'.

That is why, in the Introduction to this book, Israel was designated
as a case *sui generis*. For both the General Assembly and the Security
Council, since the Six Day War in 1967, have had the Palestine problem
constantly on their agenda – not primarily as a human rights issue but
as a major threat to world peace. None of the other cases examined in
this chapter has involved the perils of a military conflict of world-wide
possibilities as have Israel's violations of the rights of the inhabitants
in the occupied territories.

The future settlement of the people of Palestine is, of course, highly
controversial, and historically, politically and racially one of the most
emotionally charged conflicts of our generation. But that is no reason
why its essential challenge in terms of human rights should not be taken
up vigorously by all men and women of goodwill, seeking a solution
based on human dignity and governed by the rule of law.

A mission that was sent by the ILO Director-General to Israel and
the occupied Palestine territories in 1978 was led by Dr N. Valticos, a
distinguished lawyer and Assistant Director-General of the ILO and its
Adviser on International Labour Standards. He was accompanied by
Mr C. Rossillion, Chief of the Equality of Rights Branch, and by
Mr J.P. Arlès, another senior official. The mission spent from 11 to 20
April in Israel and the occupied territories. It held talks with representatives of the Israeli civil and military authorities and organisations
of employers and workers. It also met with the military commanders
responsible for administering the occupied territories and with municipal authorities, trade union leaders and other prominent persons from
the West Bank, East Jerusalem, Gaza, the Golan Heights and Sinai –
in particular, the Arab mayors of various municipal councils. With all
these and at the workplaces of various undertakings the mission had
private talks with the persons it had wanted to meet.

On the one hand the mission was afforded every facility by the
Israeli authorities to carry out its mandate and, on the other, it met an
especially favourable reaction on the part of the municipal and trade
union personalities of the occupied territories. Guided by ILO principles and objectives, the mission studied the various aspects of equality
of opportunity and treatment of the Arab workers in the occupied
territories as regards employment, conditions of work and social

benefits, as well as their trade union activities. Before passing to some specific complaints, we might look further into this carefully balanced and impartial ILO survey.[8] It states that:

> The mission realises that, because of the limited time available for drawing it up, the following account cannot claim to be complete. The mission is expecting further information and details on certain aspects of the situation, which it will consequently keep under examination. Nevertheless, the mission considers that this account gives a sufficiently representative picture of the present results of its work.

It then takes up the position of employment in Israel of Arab workers from the occupied territories. It points out that the number of workers from the occupied territories employed in Israel has fluctuated considerably over the past ten years. 'At present,' the report continues, 'the number of workers from the occupied territories in Israel is estimated at around 63,000 by the Israeli services. These workers form a fairly small though not inconsiderable part of the labour force in Israel (5 per cent), but a large proportion of the labour force in the building sector (approximately 25 per cent) and a significant percentage of the manual labour.'

When, in the course of the talks which the mission had with the leading authorities in charge of employment and labour questions, it was pointed out that equality of treatment between all workers in Israel 'was one of the fundamental principles expressly proclaimed in the policy on employment and occupation and implemented by law and collective agreements', the mission tried to form an appreciation of the gap that could exist between the law and the factual situation, for there had been recent signs of some change in the occupational structure of the active population from the territories employed in Israel. This trend, if confirmed and expanded, would imply some progress towards a more favourable distribution of the workers in jobs and occupations and towards greater job security and stability. The experience of many countries has shown that when situations persist that correspond to ethnic distinction they are likely to jeopardise social peace and justice.

It was this rather disproportionate distribution of workers from the territories in the less skilled and less well-paid jobs that might constitute one of the main reasons for the feelings of inequality among these workers, despite the declared policy of non-discrimination. Other possible explanations for these feelings were revealed to the mission by its talks with Arab workers from the territories, who seemed to be convinced that they were less protected, for example, when decisions are taken regarding dismissals. Or, again, 'they seem to feel they are treated on an equal footing as regards deductions from their wages, but unequally when it comes to the benefits to which the contributions correspond'. They feel, in fact, that for a large part, the contributions fail to serve the appropriate purposes. In particular, because they and their families live in the territories, they feel that the deduction of income tax in Israel is not designed to meet their needs in the territories. Moreover, when they think they have grounds for complaint, they seem to hesitate to have recourse to procedures which they find expensive and complicated and in which they have only limited confidence. The feeling of being treated unequally may also be due to psychological factors connected with cultural differences and the political situation. Unfamiliarity with the procedures and regulations, combined with distrust, appears to be behind most of these situations.

In the case of Palestinian workers from the occupied territories who work in Israel, there exist difficulties regarding the possibility of joining trade unions. 'At the present time,' states the mission, 'these workers do not enjoy the protection of the trade unions which exist in the territories where they live, because they work in Israel, and they are not members of the General Federation of Labour of Israel (*Histadrut*).' The mission was, however, informed that it would be possible for them to join. But the mission recalled the fundamental principles laid down in international labour standards, namely that all workers should have the right to establish and join trade union organisations of their own choosing. So efforts should also be made to increase participation by the workers from the territories in the system of workers' representation organised within the undertaking.

Turning to the situation in the occupied territories themselves, the mission was able to form an idea of some of the concrete problems presented by employment. It stated:

> In the short term, first of all, the persistent slowing down of the Israeli economy — and particularly the difficulties in the building sector — represent a threat to the employment of the workers from the territories. The mission was informed that the authorities had prepared plans or programmes to deal with this contingency. It can only recommend that the efforts in this direction be continued. A further problem, whose implications for the economy of the territories may be profound and lasting, is that of the employ-

ment of highly skilled workers, who seem unable to find adequate opportunities either in Israel or in the territories, and so have emigrated to the Arab countries in increasing numbers in recent years. This is a situation which, in the long term, might be detrimental to the qualitative standard of the labour force in the territories.

Finally, it said, the mission devoted particular attention to examining the trade union situation in the territories, for it considers that one of the decisive aspects in achieving social progress and improving life for the workers, from the point of view both of their material interests and of their dignity, *is the recognition and effective exercise of 'the right to organise'*. The visits it was able to make in the territories and the talks with trade union officers, enabled the mission to collect a certain amount of information. There are some trade unions on the West Bank which are relatively small but which seem to be able to engage in a certain number of activities. On the other hand there are unions that would seem to exist on a more or less formal basis and the mission was unable to establish whether they carried out any genuine occupational activities. In Gaza, the mission heard certain contradictory statements on the possibility of establishing trade unions, although there were assurances from the authorities that such unions could function normally if they confirmed officially their wish to do so. On this point the mission said: 'These unions should have the right to act in defence of the occupational interests of their members; and the authorities should refrain from engaging in pressure or intimidation that would unduly restrict trade union activities.'

As the mission had knowledge of a number of arrests of trade union leaders, it gave the authorities a list of leaders who had been detained either under administrative detention or after conviction by a criminal court. It asked for details as to the condition of these persons and the exact grounds for their detention. The mission received information that, of the 17 persons reported as being detained in 1976, only three had not been released, and the mission was given assurances that the remaining cases would be carefully examined shortly. The mission added:

In general the situation of persons exposed to repressive measures of any kind should be examined rapidly to ensure that there is no connection between such repressive measures and the exercise of legitimate trade union activities. If valid grounds are presumed to exist, the trade unionists should in all cases be given a fair trial as soon as possible according to established procedures and accompanied by the necessary judicial safeguards.

Generally speaking, it would appear from the foregoing report that:

(a) Measures must continue to be taken to ensure that, in accordance with the policy affirmed by the authorities, the conditions in which the Arab workers of the occupied territories are employed in Israel guarantee them in all cases – both in law and in practice – equality of treatment as regards remuneration, conditions of work and social benefits.

(b) There should be an employment policy that fully meets the specific needs of the territories in question and provides the workers concerned with appropriate conditions of economic security, participation in decisions concerning them, and social and cultural identity.

(c) Although the mission was told that most arrested trade union leaders had been released, it urged that measures should be taken to reconsider the remaining cases, as well as trade union leaders expelled from the territories who wished to return. The attention of the authorities was drawn, *inter alia*, to *the need to avoid any act which might be deemed to restrict unduly the effective exercise of trade union rights by the workers of all the occupied territories*.

It might be added to the foregoing cautious survey that the fact of a foreign authoritarian occupation brought acute psychological, political, and legal factors to an already difficult situation and thus restricted the mission's operations. The migration of workers and the uneasy relations between two different economic, social and cultural systems were part of this disturbed context; also the uncertainties of an authoritarian government imposed against the will of the people. This aspect of the situation did not, of course, fall within the competence of the ILO, but it should not be overlooked in humanitarian terms.

We have already stressed that the infringements of human rights are basically political. It is perhaps the supreme irony that the ILO should have been the conciliatory body most bitterly condemned in certain quarters for having 'politicised' its activities. In fact, this charge was one of the contributing reasons why the United States left the ILO in November 1977, when the Conference debate over Israel's actions in Palestine was the central factor involved.[9] It does not take much imagination to see that it is the stark reality of a military occupation of Arab

lands that *is* the 'politicisation', not the legal reaction of a responsible
international body seeking to uphold the principles and objectives of its
own Constitution. The ample space given in this book to both the facts
and the law underlying the Palestine question illustrates the validity,
importance, and necessity of the vast amount of 'parliamentary' time
and energy that the whole UN system has been compelled to expend on
it.

It is when we turn to the findings of the special reports made available to the Commission on Human Rights in Geneva and to the General
Assembly in New York, however, covering some ten years of deteriorat-
ing relationships, that the more sombre details shed an unearthly light
on the dignity and freedoms of those workers whose homes, fields, and
workplaces were overrun by the invaders in 1967.

That the Israeli authorities are increasingly conscious of the mechanism of employing what is, in fact, 'foreign' labour was shown on 11
September 1978, when the Histadrut Co-ordination Committee debated
a report on the question of 'unorganised employment in Israel of Arab
workers from the territories'. The Histadrut's Secretary-General, Mr
Meshel, declared that the phenomenon of two classes of workers *should
not exist* in Israel (our italics). The Histadrut would draw the Prime
Minister's attention to this serious problem and would urge the government to take effective measures to tackle so thorny a problem. The
author of the report said that 'the conclusions deliberately avoided
dealing with the political aspects of the problem at the present stage
because of their complexity'. He added that the Histadrut considered
as 'very grave' the existence of unorganised work affecting thousands
of Arab workers, and the 'unseen collaboration between the Raises
(the suppliers of workers) and the Jewish employers – farmers,
restaurant owners and cleaning services contractors' (*Ha'aretz*, 11
September 1978).

That same week another report stated that six members of *moshavim*
from the Yamit region were each fined 500 to 4,000 Israeli pounds
and sentenced to a month's suspended prison term for one year for
having employed Bedouin workers without the Employment Service's
authorisation, and children under 14, contrary to the law. It was the
first time that Israeli citizens were brought to a military court in Gaza,
on charges of contravening the military government's orders. The
defendants explained their conduct by arguing that they could not
obtain hired workers for temporary jobs through the local labour
exchange (*Maariv*, 8 September 1978).

During an inspection campaign in the same context, carried out jointly by the Minister for Employment and the military Government of occupied territories, it was discovered that 40 Jewish farmers were employing Arab children on their farms and were grossly exploiting them (*Magellan*, 28 August 1978).

Another recent local report records that the employment by contractors and *moshavim* members in the South of hundreds of Arab children from Gaza is continuing, despite efforts by the Employment Service to put an end to it. Some 300 children travel in packed lorries from Gaza to the Paz petrol station at Ashkelon every morning. There, they are 'snatched' by local contractors and *moshavim* members. The children start arriving at the petrol station at 3 a.m. and by 6 a.m. all of them are 'settled' with jobs.

An incident recently broke out between Gaza children and a contractor, who claimed that the children had not performed the work given to them and did not therefore deserve to be paid. The children denied this and claimed their wages, a scuffle developed and the police had to intervene to restore order. It appears that the Employment Service personnel from Ashkelon and Gaza used to come to the petrol station early in the morning. They filed reports against illegal employers and sent the children back to their Gaza homes. However, for the third day running the Employment Service personnel had arrived too late, when almost all the children were settled with jobs. The children earn from 60 to 80 Israeli pounds net a day, but have no 'social benefits'. Since the opening of the academic year in Gaza the number of children employed in Israel had dropped, but several hundred were still arriving daily and find work without difficulty (*Ha'aretz*, 15 September 1978).

In fact, according to the Government Press Bureau, the employment in Israel of workers from the territories is increasingly becoming one of Israel's most difficult economic and national problems. This is due to both their part in the national work force, which has now reached 5 per cent of the total number of workers employed in the country, and to their weight in a number of economic branches.

The number of workers from the territories employed in Israel is estimated to be about 65,000 at present. They constitute 30 per cent of all construction workers, about 25 per cent of all daily workers in the agricultural branch, about 20 per cent of daily workers in the sanitary branch, hotels and porterage services, and about 7 per cent of industrial workers, while their global part in these branches attains 16 per cent. These routine details were given by the Director-General of the Employment Service, Mr Baruch Haklai, at a weekly meeting of

Jerusalem's Rotary Club, dedicated to the problem of employment of workers from the territories. He said that there was no doubt that the large proportion of workers from the territories employed in Israel resulted from the sharp demand for workers by the Israeli economy, while the employment bureaux were incapable of supplying the estimated number of 10,000 workers needed (*Ha'aretz*, 13 September 1978).

With two ethnic groups and cultures in basic conflict, it would be impossible to record the daily frictions and frustrations suffered by the Palestinian workers. For example, all the West Bank towns celebrated 'May Day' in 1978 with the exception of Nablus, which was under curfew, and workers from Jenin and Nablus did not go to work in Israel that day. Requests by local Trade Union leaders and several other public figures to organise meetings on Labour Day were turned down by the Israeli authorities on the pretext of their being 'political'.

More serious, in response to a recent ILO complaint that 'Arabs in the Territories [were] denied the right to join Trade Unions', the Head of the Histadrut's Arab Department asserted that 'Arabs from the administered territories working *in* Israel receive the same wages and social benefits as Israeli workers, even though they are not members of the Histadrut' (*Jerusalem Post*, 23 May 1978). According to another report at this time, 'the number of residents of the occupied Territories working in Israel has decreased in the last few months. There are now sixty-six thousand, compared to seventy-nine thousand three years ago'.

In an earlier examination by the ILO of the situation of the Palestinian workers in the occupied Territories,[10] the authorities reversed their earlier policy of refusing Arab workers from the occupied territories admission to Israel because of an acute shortage of labour in Israel after the 1967 war. Recruitment was officially organised through a system of labour exchanges and was facilitated by the existence of a reserve of poor and unemployed workers. There resulted a migratory movement from the occupied territories to Israel, the number of Arab workers employed in Israel rising from just over 10,000 in 1969 to nearly 70,000 in 1974. According to other sources, the proportion of the labour force meeting the needs of the Israeli economy was in fact much larger: for example, 37 per cent, if account be taken of workers unofficially recruited, or 50 per cent, including those employed in the occupied territories themselves, but engaged in production for the Israeli market.

The fall in unemployment and the rise in purchasing power in the occupied territories were seen to be due not to the development of the

local economy, but to the employment of Arab workers in Israel.
Government policy, it was claimed, was having adverse consequences,
such as the breakdown of the occupational structure and of small-
scale agriculture in the territories, as well as the appearance on the
employment market of women and of young people who had given up
school. Thus, a drain occurred on the human resources required by the
economy of the territories, which suffered from a labour shortage. This
drain on manpower was accompanied by the displacement of population. The establishment of Israeli agricultural settlements in the occupied territories, added to the appropriation of land and thus aggravated
the situation of the local population.

According to a later ILO document, the overall level of employment
inside the occupied territories in April-June 1978 was 146,700 persons.
This represented only 23 per cent of the working age population (not
all of whose members, of course, are capable of work) and less than 70
per cent of the currently employed active population of the occupied
territories. The remaining 30 per cent were employed in the Israeli
economy. Although unemployment had thus been virtually avoided,
these few data are indications of the low level of employment in the
occupied territories and the large proportion of the local active population working in Israel.[11]

This second ILO Mission, which visited Israel for two weeks in
February-March 1979, and which was given all the facilities it had
requested of the Israeli Government and had travelled widely through
the whole area, pointed out that:

> There are numerous aspects of the problem of the settlements in the
> occupied territories, not the least of which is that of international
> law. However, the specific issue which the mission looked into par-
> ticularly was that of the direct or indirect effect of these settlements
> on labour and employment problems. For the Israeli authorities,
> who justify them on security grounds, the relevance of the settle-
> ments is only very marginal as they are looked upon, in practice, as
> affecting only public land or land not suitable for cultivation . . .
> According to the Palestinians to whom the mission spoke, on the
> contrary, the settlement policy of the Israeli authorities, whose
> objectives are not solely of a military nature, has serious negative
> repercussions on the employment situation and income of the local
> population, owing to the extensive natural resources (cultivable land
> and water resources) which the authorities now control; as a result,
> problems of unemployment and shifting of small owner-farmers and

countless other difficulties have appeared, while a climate of growing insecurity is kept alive by the announcement of projects on an ever increasing scale.

Moreover, the Arab Labour Office told the ILO Director-General that Palestinian workers in the occupied territories suffered from discrimination in access to employment and occupation. Since they did not have free choice of employment they were being channelled by the labour exchanges into particular types of work. Hence, they were concentrated in such branches as agriculture, building, the canning industry, and hotels and restaurants, and in unskilled jobs which Israeli workers did not want.

It was further alleged that they were being denied access to highly technical industries (electrical, electronics, chemical and diamond industries) and that skilled jobs were kept for Israelis. Worse, Arab workers in Israel had little security in their employment, being dependent on the needs of the Israeli economy and on political decisions. In the event of mass dismissal, they stood little chance of finding new jobs in the territories. Lastly, the Palestine Trade Union Federation called attention in 1976 to the current difficulties of the Israeli economy and the threat they pose mainly to the employment of Arab workers, because the mass repatriation of unemployed Arabs causes an economic crisis in the territories. This story of discrimination against the Palestinian workers will of course be prolonged so long as the military domination over their destinies continues.

Meantime, this unhappy story of discrimination and the continued deprivation of human rights in occupied territories has been the subject of many investigations by the Special Committee on Israeli Practices which has submitted reports to the General Assembly expressing its 'profound concern about continued deprivation of human rights of the civilian population'.[12]

The Special Committee urged the international community 'to assume its responsibilities *to end the occupation*, thereby safeguarding the most fundamental of human rights', and recommended the establishment of a suitable mechanism to safeguard the rights of the population 'who have been exposed for such a long time to military occupation', in view of the 'serious deterioration in the situation of detainees'.

Perhaps, to conclude this section of the present survey, a general observation would not be out of place. In the words of the Special Committee, the Israeli policies and practices had provoked a pattern of resistance on the part of the civilian population and had produced 'an ever-increasing prison population'. Prison conditions had continued to deteriorate and persons under interrogation were ill-treated. But because of Israeli refusals to allow it access to the territories, the UN inquiry group had over the years elaborated a system of monitoring information, which was now of a type regarded as 'unimpeachable'. The Committee recorded that 'the civilian population does not enjoy any protection whatsoever against human rights violations by the occupying Power', and 'the essential provisions of the Geneva Convention on the protection of civilians under military occupation are being flouted by the Government of Israel as a matter of policy'.

It is not surprising, therefore, that, when the Commission on Human Rights opened its recent session in Geneva on 12 February 1979, its first substantive action was to send a telegram to Israel calling for an end to 'systematic torture' of Palestinian detainees and repressive policies in occupied territories. The move was proposed by Pakistan, and approved by 19 votes in favour to 3 against (Australia, Canada, and the United States).

To sum up, a report prepared for the Jordanian Government by the economics department of the Jordanian Royal Scientific Society outlines five main areas where Israel has tightened its links to, and its control of, the physical and human resources of the occupied West Bank. These are the annexation of Arab land for use by Israeli settlers; the increasing Israeli dependence on the water resources of the West Bank; the Israeli economy's growing reliance on cheap Arab labour; the evolution of the West Bank as Israel's biggest trading partner after the United States; and the attempt to manipulate electricity generation and supply so as to forge closer links between itself and the occupied areas.[13] This report continues:

> These Israeli actions can be put in another way. Israel is utilising three factors of production – labour, land and capital – all originating in the West Bank and exploited by Israel in a variety of forms and in a deliberate manner. It has always been the dream of Israel to link the two economies in a way to enable Israel to reap what benefits it can from the resources of the West Bank.

One result of this, the report suggests, is that the West Bank's own economy is not moving ahead, as illustrated by the fact that the total number of workers inside the West Bank declined from 99,900 in 1970 to 92,600 in 1976 (according to Israeli figures). Even the earnings of the Arab workers in Israel are often returning to Israel in the form of payments for Israeli exports to the West Bank. In 1977, Israel took about 62 per cent of West Bank exports and provided 90 per cent of its imports. The East Bank of the Jordan, in contrast, took only 37 per cent of West Bank exports and provided a minuscule 2 per cent of its imports. Thus, the report concludes: 'The West Bank offers Israel a captive market totally dependent on developments in Israel and incapable of standing on its own feet.'

Meanwhile, in Washington DC, a letter of appeal was signed by prominent Americans and sent in December 1978 to President Jimmy Carter and Secretary of State Cyrus Vance, by the Palestine Human Rights Campaign, calling attention 'to recent accounts that have appeared in the US media, which have recorded a wave of intensified human rights violations against Palestinians on the West Bank'. Specifically, it cited the arrest and interrogation of seven students at Bir Zeit University and also seven members of the Christian Orthodox Club of Ramallah, and the demolition of workers' homes near Nablus and Ramallah.

About the same time, also, a more detailed report was published in the United States by the *Journal of Palestine Studies* on 'Israeli Deportation of Palestinians from the West Bank and Gaza Strip, 1967-1978'. It was compiled for the American Friends Service Committee in 1977 and updated in 1978. The report resulted from extensive research to determine the extent of the problem of expulsion. Its main portion is an itemised list of 1,151 Palestinians expelled from their homeland since 1967, noting each name with town, age, occupation and the circumstances surrounding the expulsion. (*Palestine Human Rights Bulletin*, No. 13, January 1979.)

Southern Africa

The white minority government of South Africa accepted in principle in May 1979 far-ranging recommendations that would lessen some of South Africa's job segregation. These recommendations are contained in a 60-page report which was made public after two years of study by a 14-member Commission headed by Nic Wiehahn, a white South African professor and labour expert. Labour Minister Stephanus Botha said that the Government approved the concept of free association, which would allow black unions to participate *for the first time* in collective bargaining in South Africa; and that the Government accepted, among other proposals, an end to the system of reserving skilled jobs for whites. In practice, however, many jobs would continue to be reserved for whites because of collective bargaining agreements.

This Government Commission urged that, because of a labour short-age, Parliament should give black workers equal pay for equal work, the right to join unions, and training for skilled jobs. One black labour leader said that this was a 'very great victory for our struggle', whereas the white Confederation of Labour warned the Minister to be very care-ful before he decided to take the rights away from white labour organisations in South Africa. The recommendations said nothing, of course, about giving South Africa's twenty million blacks the same political rights as the four-and-a-half million whites, including citizen-ship and the vote. Yet the plan would obviously have broad implica-tions for organised black labour, thus obtaining a mild form of political and economic power through their unions. And it might eventually even become a strong force for later changes in the apartheid system.

It is against this quite recent change in the Republic's stance on cer-tain limited trade union rights in South Africa – which is still to be put into legislative form – that the long drawn-out struggle against apartheid and its denial of basic human rights can best be viewed. These cosmetic reforms in trade union law hardly scratch the surface of the evils that apartheid has inflicted on the African peoples. So we must look at that aspect first. For, as a system which seeks to regulate *every* aspect of human relations on racial lines, apartheid has affected all spheres of political, economic, social and cultural life in South Africa. The violations of personal liberties and civil rights to which it has given rise, as well as the effects it has had in the fields of education, culture and sports have received wide publicity. But consequences of apartheid in the field of workers' rights need special emphasis because they are even more far-reaching than in other fields. The livelihood of millions of workers and their families is directly at stake. For this reason the ILO is intimately concerned about the problem of apart-heid and has played a continuously vigorous part to counteract this policy.

While cases of racial discrimination occur in other parts of the world, it is the systematic and official character of apartheid which makes South Africa unique in the world today. The discovery, towards the end of the nineteenth century, of considerable mineral wealth, which led to the industrial expansion which characterises South Africa today, made necessary the availability of a large labour force to develop these resources. There thus developed a form of master and servant relation-ship in which the whites controlled all the levers of political and econo-mic command, while the Africans supplied the basic labour force needed both in the mines and on the whites' farms. This fundamental inequality was extended through legislation to all aspects of the country's economy and applied especially to fields involving industrial relations and labour. With the advent to power in 1948 of the National Party, *which has ruled South Africa ever since*, racial discrimination has been further and further entrenched in a systematic application of the Government's policy.

The cornerstone of this policy is the system of race classification which was introduced by the Population Registration Act 1950, under which the whole population is classified into a number of rigid racial categories. It is a person's racial classification and not his individual merits or qualifications which determines what rights he may exercise. This system has had decisive consequences in the labour field, since the policy and law are that a person's racial category determines what education and training he is entitled to receive and what jobs he may perform. Whatever cosmetic changes may be introduced under Western and United Nations pressure, these laws remain the key element of the overall policies of the Government, which it seeks to enforce as rigidly as it can.

This policy is known as 'separate development' and is aimed at dividing up South Africa into a territorial unit reserved for white control and some nine or ten small areas set aside for the Africans, established on a tribal basis and referred to as 'Bantu homelands'. The area controlled by the whites (about 20 per cent of the population) amounts to 87 per cent of the whole territory of the Republic, including all the main urban and industrial areas; whereas the Africans (about 70 per cent of the population) are to have only 13 per cent of their national territory. The government's intention has clearly been stated as being that 'for all eternity, as long as we exercise the authority, we stand for the domination of the whites in the white areas'. However, in practice, the policy results in millions of Africans living and working permanently in the 'white areas', and often having only the remotest connection with their areas of tribal origin, thus being reduced to the status of foreigners within their own country.

Yet, the rapidly expanding economy is becoming ever more dependent on African labour, and the number of Africans in the white areas is steadily growing. A National Party MP has argued for this policy of 'separate development' in the following terms:

> Just as someone overseas who sells machinery to us is supplying a commodity, so the Bantu labourer is supplying a commodity to us.

But that does not mean that we are integrating them into our economy as individuals . . . As soon as the Opposition understands this principle that it is labour we are importing, and not labourers as individuals, the question of numbers will no longer worry them. . . It makes no difference whether one or 5,000 or 5,000,000 Bantu come here to supply labour and then return to their homeland.

Where does this barbarous doctrine stand in the light of the declaration of Labour Rights, going back to the Treaty of Versailles of 1919, namely, that 'Labour is *not* a commodity?' And what has become of the much broader terms spelled out in the Universal Declaration of 1948 (dealt with in earlier chapters), and accepted by the whole civilised world? As regards the ILO's reaction, it may be recalled that South Africa was among the founder members of the ILO and had earlier made important contributions to its work; but the development of the pernicious policy of apartheid imported such fundamental contradictions between that policy and the principles on which the ILO is based – particularly after the emergence of a large number of independent countries on the African Continent to membership of the ILO – that matters came to a head in 1963, when the delegates from a number of countries expressed their determined opposition to the presence of a South African delegation at the International Labour Conference.

The Governing Body, 'acting as spokesman of the social conscience of mankind', outlined the case against apartheid in the labour field and solemnly reaffirmed the principle that 'all human beings, irrespective of race, creed or sex, have the right to pursue both their material well-being and their spiritual development in conditions of freedom and dignity of economic security and equal opportunity'. It emphatically condemned the racial policies of South Africa and called upon the Government of South Africa to take a number of specified measures necessary to bring the policy of apartheid to an end.

What was the immediate result? Faced with the growing pressure of condemnation by the other members of the ILO, the South African Government informed the Director-General on 11 March 1964 of its decision to withdraw from membership of the Organisation, thus breaking off an association which had lasted since the Union of South Africa became a founder member in 1919, with the signing of the Treaty of Versailles by its two famous Generals, Botha and Smuts.

That was not the last, of course, of this sordid story of man's inhumanity to man; so we must pass on to consider the violent opposition to apartheid which has mounted, year by year, within the UN system as a whole. There are many cases where there are deprivations of human rights by governments in other areas of the world, of course, but few have raised it to the level of a matter of state policy. Quite clearly the southern Africa situation – centred on South Africa – presents a unique case where the deprivation of human rights is fundamental government policy. And, as we noticed above, apartheid has been developed as a philosophy of modern government and as an economic and social order ever since the United Nations took over its 'impossible' global responsibilities in 1945. Ever since its foundation, therefore, South Africa has been the heaviest burden inflicted not merely on the twenty million or more black and coloured individuals whose country it is, but on the world community at large, whose white people number only one in seven.

The Working Group of Experts, charged with the investigation of human rights in southern Africa, was originally established in 1967 by the UN Commission on Human Rights to examine charges of torture and ill-treatment of prisoners – for example, detainees in policy custody – in the Republic of South Africa. ECOSOC then asked the Group to investigate infringements of trade-union rights in South Africa. (We shall come back to these later.) This mandate was later extended by resolutions of the Council and the Commission on Human Rights, which, in 1975, decided that the Group should survey further the policy of apartheid and racial discrimination in Namibia and Southern Rhodesia, as well as the private jail and farm-jail systems and also the 'homelands' policy and its effects on the right of self-determination. So, for over a decade, a careful and exacting investigation of all aspects of human rights has been pursued in southern Africa, reporting regularly to the principal UN organs, for the whole world to know about.

In the course of these twelve years, thousands of witnesses have been interviewed by the UN Group, and innumerable reports have been assembled on a vast range of topics. Dozens of governments in Africa and beyond have co-operated, and an increasing list of violations of human rights law has been itemised and recorded. Nothing like this supreme international effort has ever been conceived or accomplished before. There is no going back.

It is not always realised that UN investigations of this order of magnitude proceed on the strict basis of international law, and not on political grounds. In preparing their periodical reports the Working Group has acted on various international instruments establishing standards on human rights within its purview, including the UN Charter, the Universal Declaration and the Nuremberg principles, as

well as on major International Covenants on economic and political
rights and the Optional Protocol which entered into force on 23 March
1976. To these must be added the International Covenant on the Suppression and Punishment of the Crime of Apartheid, which came into
force on 18 July 1976.

The quality and representative character of this investigating Group
are obvious from its current membership, namely: Kéba M'Baye (Sene-
gal), Chief Justice of the Supreme Court (Chairman); Branimir Jankovic
(Yugoslavia), Professor of International Law, Belgrade; Amjad Ali
(India), Member of Parliament, New Delhi; Annan Arkyin Cato (Ghana),
Counsellor, Ghana Mission to the UN; Humberto Diaz Casanueva
(Chile), Professor of Spanish American Literature, Columbia University;
and Félix Ermacora (Austria), Professor of Public Law, Vienna.

One of the most bitter hardships imposed over the last 30 years on
the victims of apartheid (that is, separate development) are the passbook laws. Blacks and coloureds consider South Africa's passbook system one of the most humiliating of discriminations. For example, a
total of 216,112 black men and 33,918 black women were arrested in
South Africa in 1976 alone for passbook irregularities or for being in
areas not authorised in their books.

A network of pass laws under the Urban Areas and Masters and
Servants Acts have compelled each 'native' to carry up to a dozen different passes. Many illiterate blacks may not be able to read them. The
'regular' passes include:

1. residential or site permit
2. lodger's permit
3. night pass after 11 p.m.
4. permit to seek work
5. copy of contract with employer
6. casual labourer's licence (if that is his work)
7. registration certificate, if no contract of service
8. temporary visitor's permit
9. exemption certificate, if he is *not* required to carry a pass.

Although the 'citizens' of Transkei now carry their 'national' passports, restrictions governing the new document are the same as for the
old. As they did with the passbooks, employers sign the passports every
month — the white regime's guarantee that the documents are valid.
Yet, once outside the Transkei borders, the 'citizens' find themselves
foreigners within their own country — South Africa! Transkei was

separate-development multiplied.

Apartheid has been described historically as an 'accumulative and purposeful system of racial containment'. Its components fall into four distinctive categories: (a) racial prejudice and discrimination; (b) racial segregation and separation; (c) economic exploitation of natural and human resources; and (d) legal oppression and police terror. Its proponents would have the world believe that genuine apartheid is merely 'racial separation', terror being simply a means to perfect the end! But, in reality, it is the terror, whatever the intentions of its perpetrators, that has become the true apartheid – perhaps its most indestructible component – and on which it must depend for its continuance.[14]

Legalised racial discrimination is a public act of humiliation, taken to the disadvantage of its victims, and serves three main social objectives, namely: (1) to denigrate the capabilities of Africans; (2) to sustain among Europeans a communal sense of superiority; and (3) to protect the status and jobs of Europeans on the basis of colour. It would be impossible to summarise, moreover, under the Terrorism and Anti-Communism Acts, how horrendous have been the implications of 30 years of consistent terrorism inflicted *on* the black workers in their own land by the white architects of this police state. UN Secretary-General, Kurt Waldheim, summed up the present position when he said:

What we have today in South Africa is a dangerous confrontation of races, caused by the exclusion of the black population from the political life of the country and by the imprisonment, detention and banning of many of their acknowledged leaders. In my view the earlier Security Council recommendation for a National Convention remains valid today, offering a constructive approach for a peaceful and lasting solution.

Unfortunately, the convening of such a National Convention in South Africa seems as far off as ever. Meantime, in 1978, an out-flanking political movement began to be evident in negotiations between five Western powers – Britain, the United States, France, West Germany and Canada – and (then) Prime Minister Vorster over the liberation of South-West Africa, where the same evils prevail. The near likelihood of an independent Namibia, under the transitional adminis-tration of the United Nations itself, thus freeing Namibia from South Africa's thraldom, would plainly be a major influence in establishing democracy in Southern Rhodesia, too; and, conversely, it would be a step towards the gigantic change-over yet required of South Africa itself.

In other words, in southern Africa we are awaiting political solutions of
a fundamental kind; all of which fall outside the scope and purpose of
the present book.

Reverting, however, to the 'cosmetic' concessions mentioned at the
beginning of this section, which were made in May 1979 by Pretoria's
white minority Government in allowing some black unions to participate for the first time in collective bargaining, a contemporary editorial
comment might seem to indicate a modicum of progress:

> As many industrialized countries have demonstrated, unions can be
> more effective than political parties in determining such matters as
> costs, profits and the distribution of wealth. They can also be power-
> ful in politics. Union membership could be more useful to South
> Africa's blacks than the vote.[15]

Soviet Union

The invidious term 'blackmail' was quoted in the previous chapter as
emerging from the lips of some experienced diplomats, reacting to the
walk-out of the United States in 1977, alleging that the ILO had been
selective in its discussions and was 'politicised' in favour of the communist countries. The supreme irony of this ignominious retreat of the
West's most vocal defender of human rights was compounded two
years later when (with the US delegation still in limbo), the Soviet
Union was seen defending itself vigorously before the Governing Body
of the same ILO on the grounds that the complaint being levied against
it was a 'political creation of the West', instigated by a 'group of mal-
contents exploited by the Western press.'[16]

Actually, there were three areas in which Soviet policy, not for the
first time, had clashed with ILO principles; namely, the position of
forced labour and of certain practices on the collective farms, which we
shall first consider briefly and in summary form; and, more significantly, the setting up of a so-called 'Free Trade Union', which became
the topic of world criticism and controversy. What some Geneva offi-
icials have since been asking is whether the Soviet Union will resort to
the same 'blackmail' tactics which, in retrospect, so demonstrably failed
to shake either the integrity or capacity of the Organisation as a result
of the precedent set by the US in 1977.

Coming first to the Forced Labour Convention, ratified by the
USSR in 1956, the ILO Committee of Experts on the Application of
Conventions and Recommendations has for a number of years drawn
attention to 'shortcomings' in its implementation. The Committee's

scrutiny has been directed particularly to Soviet 'anti-parasite' legislation and to restrictions upon workers' freedom to *leave* collective farms. What is then so objectionable in all this?

Under laws introduced in the early sixties in the various Republics, persons who are considered to be evading socially useful work and to be leading an anti-social, parasitic way of life, could be directed to employment by the administrative authorities. These laws were repealed in 1975, following criticism by the ILO Committee of Experts. However, the scope of penal provisions on vagrancy and begging was extended to cover also 'persons leading over a prolonged period of time any other parasitic way of life'. But the relevant ILO Committee has pointed out that these provisions could well constitute a means of compulsion to work, so they have called for amendment of that Soviet law, too.

The Committee of Experts has also pointed out that members of collective farms were allowed to terminate their membership only with the consent of the collective management. As long as they remained members of a collective farm, they were not issued with a passport or a workbook, both of which were prerequisites for taking up other employment. They thus remained tied to the collective farm, unless given permission to leave. Then, in April 1975, regulations were approved under which collective farmers were issued workbooks. The Committee of Experts noted, however, that these workbooks were to be kept at the management office and were to be handed to the worker only if and when he ceased to be a member of the collective farm. Since the production of the workbook is required for taking up other employment, the Committee therefore has asked the Government to amend the collective farm rules to provide expressly that membership may be brought to an end by the individual member's unilateral decision, subject to reasonable notice.

It was while these pressures on the Soviet Government were continuing that trade unions in the USSR opened up a major confrontation with the ILO. The USSR had, in fact, ratified the Freedom of Association and Protection of the Right to Organise Convention (1948) as long ago as in 1956. Needless to stress, it was when the Committee of Experts first examined the situation that it observed that trade union rights in the USSR were subject to a number of restrictions, which were not compatible with the Convention. We need only pin-point some of these relevant to the present discussion. One of them was that legislation did not permit workers to establish organisations of their own choosing. It was also prohibited to establish federations outside the existing trade union movement. Finally, by virtue of article 126 of the

Constitution, the Communist Party was to be the 'leading core' of all organisations of working people, so the Committee concluded that all organisations were placed under the direction of the Communist Party, and that it was legally impossible to set up an organisation of workers *independent of the Party*.

That was a tough nut to crack! The Government maintained that it was necessary, in evaluating compliance with the Convention, to take account of economic and social conditions *and of their historical evolution*, and that the laws and practice of the USSR effectively guaranteed the rights provided for in the ILO Convention. Following this line, the Committee of Experts noted with satisfaction that the removal of the obligation for trade unions to *register* with the Central Council of Trade Unions was a step in the right direction. Other issues, however, remain unresolved.

When, then, in January 1978, the World Confederation of Labour (WCL) and the International Confederation of Free Trade Unions (ICFTU) were informed of the creation of a trade union in the USSR to defend the interests of the workers, 'in response to the need for the workers themselves to have an instrument that is independent of the Party and of the State, with a view to exercising their inalienable right to freedom of association', the battle was joined. The Soviet authorities had reacted immediately and the workers who set up the 'free' trade union were arrested. Vladimir Khlebanov, for example, was arrested by police officers in a Moscow underground station during the night of 7 February 1978 and, on the same date, Valentin Poplavsky was arrested at his home, and Varbara Kutcherenko was confined to a psychiatric hospital. The WCL and the ICFTU had all the facts.

In its communication to the ILO, the ICFTU protested against 'the repressive measures taken against the founder members of the Workers' Free Trade Union' and stated that on 20 May 1977 eight workers, whose names were listed, signed an open letter explaining that they had all been dismissed from their work, arrested or confined to psychiatric hospitals for having criticised or denounced the abuses of the heads of the enterprises where they worked. They also cited the names and occupations of 35 other workers, who had been subjected to various repressive measures after they had lodged complaints against bad working conditions, insufficient wages, or the lack of safety at work.

Since all other means of having their situation remedied had failed, these workers had decided to set up a trade union, so on 1 February 1978, they published the provisional by-laws of the 'Workers' Free Trade Union Association', accompanied by an appeal to the ILO and to international trade union organisations. The ICFTU listed the names of the '43' and gave details of their treatment. For example, among others, Valentin Poplavsky was condemned by a Moscow municipal court to one year in a prison camp for 'parasitism', from which it was clear that to express one's views as a worker could lead to prison or to the psychiatric hospital.

But what came out even more clearly was the revelation that it was impossible to create a trade union organisation independent of the state and of the Party. Furthermore, the fact of having wanted to create such a trade union has led to a number of workers being put into prison. The complainants could not take up the political angle, however; but they concluded that the Conventions on freedom of association had been violated, and requested the urgent despatch of a mission of 'direct contacts' with the USSR authorities.

Information compiled by the always alert Amnesty International confirmed that, on the basis of documents issued by a group of unemployed Soviet workers, they had associated together to protest against violations of their rights of freedom of expression. The group's documents listed dozens of cases of workers who had been confined to psychiatric hospitals in recent years for persisting in lodging complaints against their work superiors. According to the documentation supplied, it was early in December 1977 that details became known outside the USSR of a sizeable group of workers who had associated together in Moscow to protest collectively against the authorities' refusal to meet their complaints of wrongful dismissal from work and other employment-related abuses. (See Appendix E.)

The group stated that it had begun its existence through an 'accidental meeting' of unemployed workers who had come to Moscow to press their complaints in person at the offices of the highest party, the Government and the legal authorities. Some of these workers had met in the public reception rooms of these official offices and decided to press their complaints collectively. The first known collective action as a group was in May 1976 when Nadezhda Ivanovna Gaidar, an engineer from Kiev, went with a complaint to the Procurator General's Office. She was taken to a psychiatric hospital and later transferred to another similar hospital in Kiev, from which she was released after two months.

Vladimir Khlebanov acted as the principal spokesman and organiser of the group from its inception. When he worked as a foreman at the Bazhanova coal mine in the Donetsk region (in the Ukraine), he had tried in 1960 to start an independent trade union among coalminers at his mine, but the local authorities called this 'anti-Soviet activity' and

stopped his efforts. He was dismissed in 1968 for refusing, *inter alia*, to
send his men on jobs where he believed safety standards were not met;
and he wrote a letter of protest about the high accident and fatality
rate at the mine. When he protested against his dismissal, he was ruled ment
ill and confined to a maximum security psychiatric hospital. After his
release he was unable to obtain work because his personal labour book note
that he had been 'dismissed in connection with arrest'. He was rearrested
and confined to a psychiatric hospital for two months in February 1977.

Other members of the group were subjected to similar acts of official
repression in 1976 and 1977. The aforementioned Valentin Poplavsky,
one of the most active members of the group, was detained at the reception room of the Central Committee of the Communist Party and
'within one hour' was sentenced to 15 days in jail. No wonder that, on
7 November 1977, 33 workers signed a 'collective complaint' addressed
to the Soviet authorities *and the foreign press*, asking that the authorities create a commission to investigate treatment of the complaints. The
signatories said that they had been dismissed from their jobs for criti-
cising abuses by their work superiors and that, in contravention of
Soviet laws, the authorities were passing on their formal complaints to the
very officials named in the complaints, and this facilitated acts of
repression by the latter.

Hence, at a press conference in January 1978, the group announced
its intention of forming an 'independent trade union'. Its spokesmen
stated that 200 workers had agreed to join the body and showed foreign
correspondents a list of some 100 candidate members, most of whom
were unemployed. Still uncertain as to the name, they thought it
would be called the 'Trade Union for the Defence of Workers'. They
had decided on this step because of the ineffectiveness of the country's
established trade unions, which were 'government-controlled', and they
could not do anything individually, so had to act together. They stated
that they were going to ask the ILO to 'recognise' their independent
trade union. However, as stated above, the approach to the ILO could
only legally be effected by one of the recognised world trade union
organisations already associated with the ILO.[17]

How did the Government of the Soviet Union respond to these
specific changes — and many similar detailed complaints — when trans-
mitted to them by the ILO, in the same form in which they had been
received in Geneva? It might be recalled that the USSR had ratified the
Freedom of Association and Protection of the Right to Organise Convention of 1948, and the Right to Organise and Collective Bargaining
Convention of 1949. In its reply of 9 November 1978, the government

stated that the allegations in the complaints were completely unfounded. The government went on to state that 'the right of workers to organise collectively and the freedom of action of trade unions in the USSR are guaranteed by the country's Constitution and are exercised in practice consistently and scrupulously'. Moreover, trade unions act in conformity with their by-laws and take an active part in the administration of public affairs and in the resolution of economic and socio-cultural problems. They also enjoy extensive rights as concerns the defence of the workers' interests, since they have at their disposal the legal labour inspection services.

The government further declared that the persons to whom reference had been made in the communications had 'no connection either with the trade unions or with the defence of the occupational interests of the workers, whom they do not represent'. The government added that 'it is perfectly obvious that the letters from the WCL and the ICFTU are based on notoriously inaccurate information, the only effect of which could be to distort the truth and mislead public opinion'. Their examination by the ILO was accordingly illegal and inadmissible, and therefore the government expected the ILO to take steps to prevent the Organisation from becoming involved in an insidious political campaign which might be severely detrimental to the Organisation's action in defence of the rights of the workers.

As can well be imagined, given the balanced and highly expert composition of the ILO's Committee on Freedom of Association, its recommendations in April 1979 to the ILO's Governing Body (on which the USSR has representatives) put the Soviet Union 'on the spot' for a severe cross-examination before world opinion. The Committee considered that it was dealing with receivable complaints alleging facts which, if proved, could be deemed to jeopardise the free exercise of trade union rights. In accordance with procedure and practice followed in earlier cases, it had the duty to examine the substance of the allegations that had been made. And the Soviet Union was obliged by its commitments under the Conventions it had ratified to reply to the Committee as to the substance of the case, especially as the complainants had supplied detailed information as to the identity of the persons affected, the dates of their arrest or confinement to hospital, and in some cases the places where they were still detained or confined in psychiatric hospitals.

The Committee therefore rejected the Soviet contention that the persons mentioned in the complaints did not represent the workers; but that 'when a complaint contains precise allegations, the Committee is of the opinion that the reply of the government concerned should not be limited to observations of a general nature'. The ILO Governing Body, after listening to the defence put up by its Soviet members, put the ball vigorously back into Moscow's court, requesting the government to provide detailed information concerning: (i) the allegations that it is impossible legally to create in the USSR a trade union organisation independent of the state and of the Party; and (ii) the facts alleged by the complainants concerning the arrest or confinement in psychiatric hospitals of the founders or members of the association mentioned in the complaints.

As stated earlier, the battle is joined in one of the most history-making vindications of human rights — with the United States, curiously enough, still on the sidelines.

Tunisia

In September 1978 an Amnesty International research observer was sent to Tunis to observe the trial before the State Security Court of 30 trade union leaders arrested in January and February 1978 on a wide range of charges relating to a one-day general strike on 26 January 1978. The strike, the first of its kind in Tunisia since independence in 1956, produced armed clashes between the strikers, the police and the armed forces, and many arrests followed. Twenty-four defendants received sentences ranging between ten years' hard labour and six months' imprisonment. The remaining six were acquitted.

Unfortunately, the woman observer was not permitted entry into the court room to observe the proceedings. She concluded, however, from information obtained from those who did attend the trial, that 'the rights of the defence in this trial were gravely abused'. In particular she made the following criticisms:

(a) Despite the fact that the dossier against the defendants was over 4,000 pages long, the court granted the defence lawyers only two weeks to study it;

(b) One of the defence lawyers, a former Minister of Justice and former President of the Tunis Bar Association, made several submissions to the court, but the President repeatedly interrupted him and threatened him twice to withdraw. Finally he did withdraw along with all 25 lawyers for the defence. The President thereupon announced sanctions against him, banning him from the Bar for two years under a 1968 law instituting the Court of State Security.

(c) Court lawyers were appointed, but the defendants refused to continue their defence as they had been given no opportunity to consult with each other and the lawyers had had no opportunity to study the trial documents.

Amnesty International's conclusions were that, as the lawyers for the defence originally chosen by the detained trade unionists were not given time to study the case dossier, and it was obvious that the lawyers appointed by the court had only a matter of hours to read the detailed charges and no opportunity to consult with their clients, they were quite unable to act on their behalf, and this lack of consultation effectively prevented the trade unionists from having an adequate defence. In short, the proceedings fell far short of the internationally recognised standards of impartiality as set down in Article 14 of the International Covenant on Civil and Political Rights, which the Tunisian Government ratified in 1969.

But this incident was not the first of its kind, for the Tunisian Government was faced with an embarrassing request from Mr Otto Kersten, General-Secretary of the International Confederation of Free Trade Unions, for permission to give evidence in person at the trial of Mr Habib Achour, the indicted Tunisian trade union leader in August 1978. The trial concerned Mr Achour and his ten senior deputies in the UGTT (Tunisia's central trade union organization) all of whom had been detained since 28 January, two days after the general strike.

Mr Kersten's request came from the Confederation's Brussels headquarters after the alarming news that the state prosecutor had demanded the death penalty for 39 of the 101 local trade unionists on trial. Moreover, four French barristers engaged by the Confederation to attend the Sousse trial were expelled along with a barrister representing the international organisation of Arab trade unions. And so on.

Two earlier trials at Sfax had set the frame for these travesties of justice. At the first trial 22 workers from the Gafsa phosphate mines, arrested the previous November and held in detention, were sentenced to between four months and two years in prison. While at the second, twelve officials of the UGTT's regional office were accused of stocking weapons and eight were jailed for two years. The 'arsenal' consisted of some petrol bombs, iron bars, and cudgels; but was regarded as proof that the UGTT was planning a coup. Yet the defence lawyers pointed out that the weapons were for self-defence after repeated attacks on the UGTT's offices ever since Mr Achour led the unions out of their social pact with the government and began lightning strikes to improve pay and conditions.[18]

A report issued in March 1979 by the French section of Amnesty International said that jailed Tunisian labour union leaders had been tortured and some held in deplorable conditions. The report continued: 'Almost all leaders of the Tunisian labour union movement are now in prison following a general strike on January 26 of last year to protest rising prices and the Government's economic policy.' Twenty-four union leaders were sentenced to prison or forced labour for terms of between six and ten years and others were still awaiting trial. Of those imprisoned, Habib Achour, aged 66, secretary-general of the Union, was being held in deplorable conditions, as was Salah ben-Kaddour. Most of the scores of union members who appeared before the Tunisian courts were tortured, either with lighted cigarettes or club blows, Amnesty said. Some were hung by the knees from a pole and beaten.

Uruguay

Uruguay provided yet more disquieting information during the course of 1978 on treatment given to detainees arrested for political reasons than many earlier arrests of political suspects that had been carried out steadily throughout several years. Massive and simultaneous raids have been conducted, with all the characteristics of a military operation, on individuals and organisations. According to an earlier investigation by the International Commission of Jurists, the army arrested in April 1975 some 1,800 workers of the Salto Grande hydro-electric dam, which was being built jointly by the Argentine and Uruguayan governments. This massive arrest took place at the moment when the workers were leaving a meeting convened to discuss possible action to support workers' grievances on salaries and working conditions. During their detention they were subjected to ill-treatment by the army. But a strike by the workers on the Argentine side of the dam eventually forced the Uruguayan authorities to set their detainees free.[19]

Then again, some 300 workers were arrested at the beginning of November 1978, and were kept in secret places. Their families and lawyers were unsuccessful in all their efforts to find out where they were being detained and *why* they had been arrested. These detainees included former Members of Parliament, school and university teachers, doctors, lawyers, architects, and other university graduates, journalists and a large proportion of trade unionists.

Freedom of association and assembly continues to be severely restricted in Uruguay. No political activities may take place. This situation has been laconically described by the government as a 'party political recess', a euphemistic term for a ban on the functioning of political parties and on any other political activities.

Restrictions on freedom of association apply even to professional bodies. Under a Ministry of the Interior order, lists of candidates for elections to their directing boards or councils must be submitted in advance to the Minister. On 14 October 1975, for instance, the Minister ordered the Uruguayan Association of Notaries to refer to police head-quarters the list of candidates for their Board of Directors, 'in order that candidates having an ideological background incompatible with the democratic system (*sic*) be deleted from the said lists'. When this was done. the police ordered that 33 out of the 44 candidates be deleted. Among those eliminated were many who had no connection with any Marxist or left-wing party. Lawyers have not been notable as a particu-larly revolutionary sector of the population in Uruguay, but this is typical of the action taken in relation to other professional bodies.

These incidents may sound like generalities and sadly commonplace in comparison with the malpractices of certain other Latin American countries like Chile, which are constantly in the news because of their discreditable record as torturers and killers of their political opponents. But the ICJ has been more specific in investigating a number of cases, for example, reporting in one such case in 1976 that:

> Alvaro Balbi, age 34 and father of four, was arrested 29 July 1970. He was a member of the Communist Party and an employee in a trading firm. On 31 July his body was delivered to his relatives, who were forbidden to open the coffin. The family finally got a court order for a post-mortem examination, which revealed a crushed chest, scorched genitals. damaged liver, fractured left leg, fractured skull. Balbi was killed by a military unit, but his body was handed over by the Political Police in Montevideo. His father, a well-known educator, addressed a remarkable open letter to the Uruguayan President, describing the details of the case and urging an investiga-tion.[20]

The foregoing was, of course, a private investigation, but the ILO Committee on Freedom of Association has gone particularly into the abuse of trade union rights. Meeting at Geneva in November 1978, the Committee had before it: (i) a number of complaints of infringements of trade union rights in Uruguay, presented by various trade union organisations, and (ii) a complaint concerning the observance by Uruguay of the Freedom of Association and Protection of the Right to Organise Convention, 1948 (No. 87), and also the Right to Organise and Collective Bargaining Convention, 1949 (No. 98), made by a number of delegates to the 1976 Session of the International Labour Conference. Once again, that evil bureaucratic triad of delay, detention and torture raises its hydra-heads as the ILO probe proceeds into the facts of the situation.[21]

The case had, in fact, come up before the Committee on several occasions. Following a 'direct contacts' mission in Uruguay in April 1977 the Committee noted that there had been no change in the legal position of trade unions since July 1975. What had changed slightly was the factual situation. Although that of the unions affiliated to the General Confederation of Workers of Uruguay (CGTU) had improved and they were now able to perform certain internal activities (meetings, elections, etc.), the affiliates of the National Workers' Convention (CNT), which had been dissolved by the government after the change of regime in 1973, appeared to have remained to a large extent inactive. Many of their leaders were under arrest, had left the country or had been dismissed. The premises of certain of these unions were under police control, surveillance or closed. The extent of recognition of the unions of CGTU and their leaders depended on whether they were on good terms with the employers or their public administrative services. Unions affiliated to the CNT did not appear to be recognised.

'Normalisation' of occupational organisations, in the Government's opinion, had to be analysed within the broader framework of the political and institutional normalisation of the country. In this respect the Committee emphasised that, although respect for freedom of association was closely bound up with respect for civil liberties in general, it was nevertheless important to distinguish between the recognition of freedom of association and questions relating to a country's political evolution. Neither should there be confusion between trade unions' performance of their specific functions, that is, the defence and promotion of the occupational interests of workers, and the possible pursuit by certain of their members of other activities having nothing to do with trade union functions.

The Committee was also concerned at the slowness of the judicial procedure concerning detained trade unionists. The prolonged detention of trade unionists without being promptly tried could constitute a serious handicap to the exercise of trade union rights. Of the 19 trade unionists whom representatives of the Director-General had been able to meet or whose files he had been able to examine during his mission to Uruguay in April 1977, 15 still awaited trial late in 1978 — in some cases for several years, and only three had been provisionally released.

Complainants had made statements regarding conditions of detention and the right of defence. At first, civil lawyers could carry out their functions and defend prisoners, but this situation had deteriorated. Lawyers were arrested and accused, for example, of complicity with the prisoners; others had been threatened and had left. Those who were released could no longer exercise their profession.

As for the detained workers, they were informed, often after a lengthy imprisonment, that they must choose a lawyer within 48 hours. Having no contact with the outside world, they were obliged to accept a lawyer appointed on their behalf so that the trial was not delayed further. One representative of a complainant organisation, who was arrested in 1973 and again in 1976, described the torture to which he had been subjected, and he alleged that all prisoners were tortured. Other allegations referred to cases of ill-treatment suffered by imprisoned trade unionists. The ILO Committee had therefore stated its strong disapproval of vexations or brutality inflicted on any prisoners and so pointed out to the Government the importance which it attached to the giving of specific instructions and the imposition of exemplary penalties in order to guarantee that no detained person was subject to ill-treatment.

Conclusions

The reader will have noted, in reviewing so many actual cases of labour rights violations across the globe — of which the foregoing are but samples and by no means definitive — that no rule-of-thumb formula could describe so many tragic emergencies. Nor has any attempt been made in the preceding pages to shape the varied evidence adduced into a set or formal pattern. Obviously, a considerable range of documentation has been surveyed to furnish the facts in issue on each separate case and, as indicated in the text itself, these have been drawn from a variety of sources.

Although, by this date, the basic principles underlying human rights are pretty well known, and the machinery within the UN system aimed at their investigation and protection has become ever more precisely defined, these nine sample 'cases' reveal that not one of the victims caught in the given national situation can be sure of his vindication or personal survival. Added to this uncertainty, not one of the countries selected — almost haphazardly — for scrutiny here will lack vocal defenders excusing the delinquent government on grounds of *force majeure* or 'national security' or on some other self-justifying pretext. But, to the victim, the issue is as individual and vital as when the legendary mountain boasted to the little mouse: 'I can roll over you, and I'd never *feel* it!' To which the mouse replied: 'But I would!'

Notes

1. UN document E/CN/4/1310 (1 February 1979).
2. ILO document, *The Trade Union Situation in Chile* (1975).
3. On 9 March 1979 the state of emergency was extended for another 6 months.
4. The full text of the 'Charter 77' Manifesto is reproduced in Appendix C.
5. ILO document GB 206/5/8 (2 June 1978).
6. International Commission of Jurists, *The Review*, No. 21 (December 1978).
7. Report III, Part A, ILO, 64th Session (1978).
8. *Actions taken on the Resolutions, adopted by ILO Conference*, 59th to 63rd Sessions (1978).
9. See the author's article 'Was Carter Trapped over the ILO?', *Contemporary Review* (London, March 1978).
10. ILO document GB 199/20/11 (2 March 1976).
11. ILO document ISBN No. 92-2-101952-7 (1979).
12. Press Release, HR/668 (23 November 1978).
13. *Financial Times* (London, 26 April 1979).
14. UN document, *Centre Against Apartheid*, Report No. 8 (1977).
15. *International Herald Tribune* (5 May 1979).
16. Quoted in *International Herald Tribune* (7 April 1979).
17. ILO document GB 209/6/6 (1979).
18. *The Times* (London, 11 August 1978).
19. International Commission of Jurists, *Supplement to Report on Uruguay* (Geneva, 1976).
20. See also the author's *The New Politics of Human Rights* (Macmillan, 1978), Ch. III on 'The Mobilisation of Shame'.
21. ILO document GB 208/10/15 (14 November 1978).

Part Three

NON-GOVERNMENTAL ACTION

7 BACKING FROM TRADE UNIONS

The foregoing chapters have already shown how closely linked (within the ILO system) are the governments and the non-governmental organisations representing workers and employers. It is only possible in this chapter to select a few additional examples to those already given of how workers' rights are kept in the forefront of the world trade union movement and its national groupings.

But it must be confessed that the workers of the world are not united. Only a fraction of the global labour force is organised into trade unions – something like 200 million working people. And even these are divided by their affiliation to one or other of the three major competing international confederations. The huge American AFL-CIO is not affiliated to any.

All the same, 200 million people add up to a sizeable constituency, conferring substantial power upon those who guide their affairs. At the international level this means the International Confederation of Free Trade Unions (ICFTU), the World Federation of Trade Unions (WFTU), the World Confederation of Labour (WCL), and various international trade secretariats (ITSs) of mineworkers, metalworkers, and others.

In their short honeymoon after World War II, the Soviets, Americans and British came together to form the WFTU. But within five years, as the Cold War intensified, the Western trade unions split off and founded ICFTU. The new Confederation adopted a non-Communist, but total world line. As evidence of its global reach, 33 of the 55 delegations at its first conference represented developing countries. Our previous chapter will have shown several instances where the ICFTU has played a leading role in initiating ILO investigations into violations of workers' rights as defined by the Conventions.

The WCL is much the smallest of the three and began life as a confederation of European Catholic unions; but it has shifted in recent years to a distinctly socialist position. Accepting that the WFTU remains entrenched as an organ of the Communist nations, its voice has always been added to ICFTU and WCL protests where capitalist dictatorships have been at issue.

The representative of the World Federation of Trade Unions, for instance, reminded the UN Human Rights Commission in 1979 that his Federation had consistently denounced human and labour rights violations by the military *junta* in Chile. There had been a sharp decline in workers' living standards in Chile despite massive economic aid, because of the economic crisis precipitated by the *junta*. The cost of living in Chile during the last twelve months had risen by almost 65 per cent, he said. The vast influx of foreign money, because of the policies of the *junta*, had not brought improvements for ordinary people.

In 1975, the Eleventh World Congress of ICFTU recorded 119 affiliated union organisations (such as the TUC in Britain and the Canadian Labour Confederation) in 88 countries and covering a total membership of 53 million. In May 1978 appeared the ICFTU Development Charter under the title 'Towards a New Economic and Social Order', which insisted on the following broad questions of workers' rights:

> Workers' rights can be safeguarded only through the guarantee of
> fair labour standards. Fair labour standards may be defined as pro-
> visions assuring the workers reasonable protection and income main-
> tenance through fair wages, unemployment benefit, safety regula-
> tions, and workmen's compensation. In particular, fair labour
> standards prohibit discrimination in hiring and conditions of employ-
> ment on grounds of race, colour, creed, sex, religion, national origin
> or class. The International Labour Organisation has played a key role
> in the improvement of working conditions, the defence of trade union
> freedom, and the promotion of social justice and economic equality
> ever since its foundation in 1919. Despite its various problems, the
> ILO remains the only global organisation in which the workers have
> the right to participate together with governments and employers
> on an equal footing in matters of economic and social policy.

An AFL-CIO sponsored sea and land blockade against Chile, Nicaragua and Cuba was approved in November 1978 by the Interamerican Labour Organisation, a hemispheric group of unions with some 30 million members. Chilean Foreign Minister Hernan Cubillos said a planned international shipping boycott of Chile could strangle the economy, and was 'clear interference' in the nation's internal affairs.

However, the threat was enough, coming from so powerful a union source. The immediate result was that the Government increased some of the rights of Chilean unions, which are the traditional sources of political influence there. Union members would be able to meet without prior clearance, the Government announced in April 1979. The Government also promised a new labour code later in that year. It would even allow strikes, under limited conditions – for the first time since the coup in 1973.

There is little doubt that General Pinochet had been forced to reduce repression because of pressures such as the threatened boycott, as well as the refusal of many countries to sell arms to Chile during its tense border dispute with Argentina. Other observers realised that foreign investment in Chile had lagged because of the country's abysmal human rights image. According to several sources, Chile's image would not improve until there were real and sustained changes in the country. So the threatened South American boycott had had a multiplier effect.[1]

Note

1. *International Herald Tribune*, (5 May 1979).

8 OTHER VOLUNTARY BODIES

As indicated in the preceding chapters, the range of action by voluntary groups, which do not have the 'clout' of the major trade unions, is still considerable and is constantly growing. In this brief chapter, we can only pinpoint some of the most vocal and persistent non-governmental pressure groups, which more than fill in the gaps in public awareness left by the restraints imposed on official bodies.

Outstanding among such volunteer bodies are, of course, the highly specialised techniques employed by Amnesty International. We need only refer, in addition to what has already been said about AI, to only one typical overseas action, when in 1978, every member of the Trades Union Congress in England was asked by Amnesty International to press for immediate action over the 200 or so Russian trade unionists (mentioned in Chapter 6) who claimed that they were being subjected to persecution and brain-washing by the Soviet authorities.

In a letter to individual TUC leaders, AI suggested that union members in Britain demand an explanation from the Soviet authorities, if the TUC General Secretary received no reply to a letter he had sent to Russia asking for 'information'. AI's British trade union officer was disappointed, however, that the Labour Party itself had deferred a decision on these serious complaints against freedom of association; so AI next wrote to the British Communist Party asking it to protest to the Russians! All this domestic action, and much else, was directed to stirring the rest of the British trade union movement to intensify their protests as non-governmental bodies in the widest possible manner.

Amnesty International's report for 1978 gave, as it states, 'a depressing picture of systematic violations of basic human rights in most of the countries of the world. People are imprisoned because of their opinions, prisoners are tortured and even executed'. In fact, AI had taken action against violations of human rights in no less than 110 countries during 1978, which was the thirtieth anniversary of the Universal Declaration of Human Rights. Its report showed 'new trends in repression'. Dissidents were now being confined in mental asylums in more countries in Eastern Europe. This practice was particularly alarming, since such a system of detention gave prisoners few opportunities to appeal or to defend themselves or take any legal action.

Dealing with Western Europe, the report goes on: 'There has been a

tendency to meet terrorism with harsh anti-terrorist laws which in
themselves may open the door to violations of human rights.' And in
some Latin American and African countries terrorist acts had been
given authorisation by the governments themselves. While in several
Asian countries the rulers make use of emergency laws to 'legalise' the
preventive detention of political opponents and trade unionists. El
Salvador, for example, is the smallest republic on the mainland of
America, but has been under uninterrupted military government for 45
years. General Carlos Humberto Romero, the president, who was in-
augurated in July 1977, has now added to the political violence and
suffering of many years by causing further 'disappearances' and even the
murder and torture of the clergy.

Amnesty International's appeals are always personal, rather than
propaganda-oriented. Professor Davor Ara, for example, an archivist at
the Yugoslav Academy of Science and Arts, was one of 16 people
arrested in 1974 for allegedly planning acts against the State. He was
sent to jail for six-and-a-half years. But Amnesty International established
from sources in Yugoslavia that he was not involved in the planning or
advocacy of violence, and that he may have been convicted because of
contacts with Croatian nationalists. His imprisonment, often in solitary
confinement in an unheated cell, has induced serious illness; so AI has
been asking those concerned to write appeals for the professor's release
to President Josip Broz Tito, President of the Republic.

But less dramatic action continues all the time, coming as it does
from less specialised civic groups. From Canada, Professor J.P. Humphrey
of McGill University, told a recent seminar in Geneva, discussing education for human rights:

> Human rights are more apt to be respected in a country where there
> is an educated and alert public opinion and the citizens are actively
> concerned about their rights, than in countries where these conditions
> do not exist. And it is through non-governmental organizations that
> individual citizens can most effectively act. It is, moreover, a demon-
> strable fact that the practice of freedom and respect for human
> rights are more likely to exist in countries where there are strong
> intermediary bodies of a private character between the citizen and
> the state . . . As Lord Acton said, the existence in a country of
> independent intermediary organizations between the individual and
> the state is both a proof and a guarantee of freedom.

Their range is indeed very wide today. Private organisations, through which individuals may act, include the churches, universities, the press and other media of information. In the labour field, apart from the trade unions, there are employers' organisations, press councils and other professional associations, as well as civil liberties unions specifically concerned with the promotion of respect for human rights.

Since an educated and alert public opinion is the best guarantee of human rights, the role of the churches, the schools and universities and of the press is especially important. Educational institutions can play two roles, as Professor Humphrey pointed out, 'first in raising the general educational level of the community by their traditionally oriented courses in the law, political science, sociology and other disciplines; but nowadays more and more by offering specially oriented courses in human rights and civics'.

The judiciary and the legal profession also play an increasingly important role, since lawyers are usually members of professional organisations such as law societies and bar associations. Internationally, the International Commission of Jurists (ICJ), with its headquarters in Geneva, has been conspicuous in defending workers' rights, by organising a continuing series of missions and investigations which have left few plague-spots in the world untouched.

According to a study on El Salvador, for example, prepared in July 1978 by ICJ, a number of industrial strikes were called in October and November 1977 in support of demands for relatively modest increases in minimum wages from prevailing levels, which were about $2.48 to $3.20 a day. During the same period, two organisations of rural workers also agitated for an increase in the minimum wage for the cutting of sugar cane, coffee and cotton to a level of about $4.40. Although the El Salvadorean constitution guarantees the right to strike, 715 workers were arrested by the security forces under a new law between December 1977 and July 1978. Of these 590 were freed after, in the majority of cases, being beaten; two were assassinated and 21 just 'disappeared'.

Some non-governmental organisations, including certain civil liberties unions, throw their nets widely and are concerned with the whole gamut of human rights. Others like the Anti-Slavery Society are concerned with some particular right, such as forced labour prohibitions; or particular aspects of rights, as those organisations representing ethnic communities, like the National Association for the Advancement of Coloured People in the United States. The International Committee of the Red Cross, with a membership of 25 Swiss nationals, is quite a different kind of humanitarian operation again, supported by national sections in many countries.

Finally, it might be noted that many countries engage in practices which constitute an interference with the rights of scientific researchers and other workers. The most common practices include the imposition of restrictions on publishing research papers in journals at home and abroad; or even on reading the published works of other scientists. Worse still is the prohibition of the submission of papers to international scientific conferences or travel to and participation in such conferences and scientific communications with other scientists. The confiscation of scientific work and archives and the imposing of special terms of employment, including arbitrary dismissal and demotions resulting from the expression of ideological convictions or the expression of a desire to emigrate, can unfortunately be listed against the Communist regimes.

Added to these are the far more serious practices to which scientists are also subjected in terms of their detention, hospitalisation in psychiatric institutions, and even torture. Such interference with scientific freedom is a gross violation of the international human rights instruments described at the beginning of this book, which include freedom of association in general and 'the right to seek, receive and impart information of all kinds, regardless of frontiers', in particular. Such rights are meaningless unless scientific freedom is conscientiously protected and assured by sovereign governments.

Part Four

PROPOSED REMEDIES

9 THE UNITED NATIONS SYSTEM

One inescapable conclusion that must surely strike the reader, arising from the evidence adduced in the foregoing chapters, is that, after three decades of institutionalisation (six decades as far as the ILO is concerned), human rights have more and more penetrated the hard shell of national sovereignty. ILO Conventions, especially, have again and again reached through the frontier of the sovereign state to the individual worker or, at least, his organisation.

This does not mean to say that what are called the 'sovereign rights' of national states are not perhaps still the biggest obstacle to the fulfilment of Dr Jenks' famous phrase about the Common Law of Mankind. But it does mean that, so many breaches having already been made (due to the old procedures of the ILO and the new procedures of the UN), the modern system of sovereign states is undergoing a change as vast and drastic as that which occurred when feudalism gave way to it. But how many people realise what is happening? It is this continuing process of change that invites us to look ahead at what is both possible and desirable in the foreseeable future.

One of the most promising aspects of this global challenge to the prerogatives of the sovereign state is the glare of publicity forcing its way through the tight shutters of the prison cells and torture chambers of military dictatorships and other repressive regimes. We know more and more about *what is happening* behind the smoke-screens that recalcitrant governments depend on. The ILO and other UN bodies, with the support of NGOs (non-government organisations), like Amnesty International, have forced open the dark secrets of vindictive regimes. The mobilisation of shame has begun to work. The techniques have varied, as the foregoing chapters have revealed. Progress in upholding workers' rights has often been slow, frustrations many; but results are on the record and are coming in the whole time. Thousands of prisoners of conscience have been released and political refugees and exiles cared for.

Over 250 trade union leaders, for example, are known to have been, freed from detention over the past three years in countries in Africa, Asia, Europe, Latin America and the Middle East as a direct or indirect result of the ILO's intervention. These figures were given in a survey at the beginning of 1979 from the ILO's Governing Body's Committee on

Freedom of Association, which examines complaints of alleged violation of ILO standards on freedom of association and the right to organise. In one country, a general amnesty enabled a large number of trade unionists to be released or to return from exile. Most of the cases the Committee had dealt with had raised fundamental human rights issues, particularly in connection with the arrest, detention or exile of trade unionists. In many of them, the governments under investigation finally released the persons in question or allowed them to return from exile.

These achievements could frequently be directly linked to the Committee's action, but in other cases, its efforts had contributed to getting results from governments. The complaints examined included a variety of issues concerning the right to organise, collective bargaining and the freedom of trade unions and their leaders to carry out their functions. But more is yet to be done. So proposals to improve ILO procedures for examining complaints by the Committee will come up for decision at the next International Labour Conference.

As with all international machinery, slowness in getting results invariably brings upon the Organisation adverse criticism from a public which knows little or nothing about the obstacles in its path. That is why the earlier chapters of this book have set out the procedures leading to action, all of which require the co-operation of participating governments. But the fact that, within that short time, 250 key workers' leaders had regained their freedom, is one of the positive grounds for rejoicing.

Among other successes, the ILO Committee modestly claimed a part in the release of detained trade unionists in the Dominican Republic and the return of others from exile. A subsequent ILO mission to that country called for amending legislation to ensure application of ILO standards. In a further case concerning Chile, which had been under examination since 1973 (see Chapters 6 and 7), recent steps have been taken to permit the holding of trade union meetings. The Committee again called on the Government to ensure that new legislation conformed to the principles of freedom of association.

Even the International Organisation of Employers could claim in February 1979 that there had been 'positive developments' in government-labour relations which 'the ILO may be expected to welcome, all the more as it is very certainly to a large extent the result of the dialogue which has been carried on over the last five years between today's Government in Chile and the ILO Governing Body, not always in the easiest conditions. Successive changes and improvements in Chilean labour matters owe much to the dialogue which has been kept open'.

As regards Tunisia, where judgments had been passed against trade union leaders involved in a January 1978 strike (see Chapter 6), the Committee had pressed for clemency to be shown to those sentenced. Further information was awaited in Geneva concerning allegations of restrictions imposed on the workers' rights to join trade unions in Malaysia. And, as regards the Soviet Union, the Committee had received that government's reply to the effect that the complaints concerning freedom of association 'were based on notoriously inaccurate information'; but the Committee at once had reaffirmed that it had a duty 'to examine the substance of the allegations'. The Governing Body was, therefore, calling on that government to supply detailed information on specific allegations, and would not allow the Soviet authorities to wriggle out of the obligations it had clearly assumed by membership of the ILO and by ratification of the relevant Conventions.

In general terms, 56 changes in law and practice, to ensure compliance with ILO Conventions, were made during 1978 by 40 countries and territories in response to the ILO's expert panel, which supervises the application of labour standards. This brings the total cases of specific progress to over 1,200 since records were started 16 years ago. It certainly gives an impressive illustration of efforts made by governments to conform to the Conventions that they have ratified. Moreover, the 20-member Committee of Experts on the Application of Conventions and Recommendations recorded that the 205 ratifications registered by 33 countries for that year was the highest number since 1963. Most of them came from the developing countries. So the 60 year-old ILO has by no means neglected its primary standard-setting work, while helping to build the basic social progress which has now become part of the UN's New International Economic Order.

Reference has already been made in an earlier chapter to the principles set forth in the ICFTU's recent Development Charter, entitled 'Towards a New Economic and Social Order'. The ICFTU, in fact, has gone further and insisted that 'to give real meaning to the United Nations supervision of human rights, Member States which persistently violate basic human rights and trade union rights should be excluded from any form of UN technical or financial assistance'. Such a multilateral approach is preferable to a unilateral approach, the ICFTU contends, and shifts the initiative away from powerful countries who are indulgent to their friends and severe with their enemies. And the ICFTU continues:

Trade unions have, ever since their creation in the late nineteenth century, been internationalist in their spirit and their actions. The ICFTU and the International Trade Secretariats are proud to continue this tradition to the present day. Solidarity between trade unions is a vital means of defending trade union rights and consolidating democracy. Workers' organisations will therefore insist that governments respect the right of international affiliation; they will also insist on the established right of their international organisations in the United Nations and its specialised agencies.

The Development Charter envisages more energetic UN action and more effective UN complaints procedures for the protection of basic human rights and civil liberties. These new procedures should satisfy the following requirements:

(1) They should provide for the representation of the complainant on an equal footing with the Government against which the allegations are made;
(2) Non-governmental organisations, especially international ones, should be allowed to submit complaints;
(3) Fact-finding and other similar institutionalised activities should not require the consent of the government concerned, and the bodies involved should make decisions, even in the absence of a government's co-operation;
(4) The rules of receivability should be liberal, and the rules on the exhaustion of local remedies abandoned.

All these hopes of expected progress assume, of course, that the UN system can expand its operations in the defence of workers' rights beyond their present machinery. The creation of an international human rights court and new instruments concerning human rights protection, as well as the establishment of a United Nations *High Commissioner for Human Rights* and regional organs to deal with human rights issues, were among the topics discussed in a report by the Secretary-General submitted to the 32nd session of the General Assembly in 1978. This report was prepared in response to a General Assembly resolution on 9 December 1975 which asked the Secretary-General to update a report entitled: 'Alternative Approaches and Ways and Means within the United Nations System for Improving the Effective Enjoyment of Human Rights and Fundamental Freedoms'.

This look into the future covers the following points: strengthening the capacity of the existing UN organs, more ratifications of international covenants, possible new instruments, periodic reports by governments on human rights, fact-finding and investigation procedures, and both the establishment of an International Court on Human Rights and a High Commissioner for Human Rights or similar machinery in the field of human rights.

Will all this come about? Will 'We, the People' insist that our United Nations grows and develops to match the need with the deed? Or are these years of fruitful trial and error, of slow but steady achievement, to be thrown away or allowed to erode? Who will answer, but ourselves?

10 NATIONAL ACTION AND PUBLICITY

It obviously has not been possible to do more than record casually and in passing in these final pages the immense activity undertaken in country after country by numerous religious and other humanitarian groups, contesting the heavy hand laid by autocratic governments on workers' movements. As one example, we find in November 1978 that Chile's 31 bishops and archbishops, who have formed the principal opposition to General Pinochet's Government, met and confirmed that relations between the Catholic hierarchy and the military government had never been worse. The hierarchy, in fact, has been sponsoring hundreds of court cases against the Government on behalf of the families of those who have disappeared at the hands of the Chilean secret service.[1]

The other issue on which church and state are clashing is the Government's clampdown on trade unions. The bishops have announced that they proposed to offer training to trade union leaders to counter government attempts to make free trade union activity impossible; while the standing committee of the bishops also produced a declaration on union activity. This was because the Ministry of Labour had announced that all union leaders must say on oath that they had taken no part in politics for the past ten years and would not do so for the next ten. The Church's declaration, therefore, started from the premise that political activity was good and that union leaders could take the oath and then ignore it. This was because, in October 1978, the Minister of the Interior banned seven unions and seized their assets. The bishops argued that the Government's acts 'do not appear to correspond with the social doctrine of the Church'. And the Episcopal Vicar of east Santiago stated: 'We must defend the right of Chilean workers to free association. A profound problem is the economic model of force by virtue of which one cannot have political parties, free trade unions, free public opinion or any type of free association. I consider critical sentiment as part of a search for good. It is everybody's right.'

The church-state confrontation over the missing people is also coming to a head. The Church has presented 651 cases to the Court of Appeal, Chile's highest court, asking for a special investigating judge to be appointed.

Turning from the particular to the general in national action, it might be observed that there are no less than 38 Ombudsmen in the world today, working at the state level to investigate complaints of workers and other individuals directed against their own governments. Indeed, it is more and more recognised that one of the most effective institutions for the protection of the individual against the violation of his rights by the executive and administrative branches of his government – and sometimes even the judiciary – is the original Scandinavian institution of Ombudsman.

This office is known in some countries as the parliamentary commissioner for the protection of human rights or protection of the citizen. In the socialist countries of central and eastern Europe, for instance, some of the functions of this officer are performed by the Procurator. The institution of the Ombudsman has already spread, as stated above, to nearly 40 countries. But it may not be so well known that this recent development owes much to the United Nations, as it has been discussed at many human rights seminars organised by the Division of Human Rights.

Although there are variations from country to country, the Ombudsman is essentially an officer directly responsible to the legislature. His duty is to watch over the performance of the administration and to report to the legislature, thereby giving publicity to deficiencies and exposing neglect in the performance of duties. While the Ombudsman does not ordinarily have judicial powers (although the original Scandinavian appointment did have such powers), he receives and investigates complaints, and may also act on his own initiative.

A *Ministerio público* exists in all the Hispanic American countries and is usually provided for in the constitutions thereof, as in the case of Colombia, Ecuador, Guatemala and Venezuela. His functions in those four countries include ensuring that the administration of justice is legally correct, prompt and effective. The action of the *Ministerio público* extends to all law courts and to those of the administration as well. The head of the *Ministerio público* is the *Procurador General* who may be freely elected by the legislature or elected from a list of candidates submitted by the President of the Republic for a fixed term.

In Japan, as another case, the Civil Liberties Bureau of the Ministry of Justice and the system of Civil Liberties Commissioners (established in 1948) is composed of officials of the Ministry, while the Commissioners – numbering about 8,500 – are citizens of high moral and educational standing who are appointed for a term of three years by the Minister for Justice, upon the recommendation of mayors of cities, towns and villages. The functions of the Bureau and of the Commissioners are, in particular, to investigate cases of violation of human rights:

for instance, cases of improper search or seizure by the police. Inquiries
are usually initiated upon the receipt of complaints, numbering about
7,000 annually. The organs concerned have no authority to carry out
compulsory investigations. In most cases the Bureau and the Commissioners limit their action to giving advice or to warning the Administration, and to extending their assistance to the victims, for instance in
the form of legal aid.

Apart from the trade union organisations (Chapter 7) and the voluntary bodies mentioned above, it should not be overlooked that a considerable range of national institutes play today a direct or indirect role
in the education of public opinion towards greater awareness of, and
respect for, human rights obligations. For instance, the Indian delegate
at a recent United Nations Seminar on National and Local Institutions
for the Promotion and Protection of Human Rights, held at Geneva on
18-29 September 1978, summed up the Indian position as follows:

> Human Rights have special overtones in the field of Labour. The
> Universal Declaration of Human Rights, as also the relevant ILO
> Conventions, lay down specific obligations in this regard. These are
> spelt out in precise terms in the Indian Constitution as well. Rights
> to freedom of association, to social security, to just and favourable
> conditions of work, to adequate remuneration are some of these
> rights. These are ensured to the workers and protected to the extent
> possible through a series of labour legislation (*sic*) enacted over the
> years, especially since Independence. A unique feature of labour laws
> in India is that they are formulated on the basis of the widest con-
> sultation of the interests concerned, i.e. Government, Employers
> and Workers.[2]

He goes on to point out that this tripartite consultation machinery
at the national level includes the Indian Labour Conference, the
Standing Labour Committee, and the Industrial Committee. Such agencies exist at the state level too. Significantly, too, employers and workers
are associated not only in the formulation of labour laws but also with
their implementation. Tripartite Advisory Committees have been established in this regard under the enactments concerned, like those per-
taining to health, safety and welfare, social security, and wages. And he
emphasises that bodies such as these, which include non-officials and
advise the Government in the formulation of labour policy and keep a
watchful eye on its implementation, are the promoters and guardians of
human rights in the labour field. In essence, they partake of the character

and *perform the functions of national or local institutions in the field of human rights concerning labour*.

In addition, special agencies such as labour courts and industrial tribunals have been set up under Indian labour law with functions and jurisdiction under the respective laws. Vigilance Committees are provided under the Bonded Labour Systems (Abolition) Act 1976, which is aimed at the abolition of the bonded labour system with a view to preventing the economic and physical exploitation of weaker sections of the people. Besides officials, these Vigilance Committees include social workers and credit institutions. Their functions comprise, apart from advising authorities on implementation of the Act, keeping an eye on offences occurring under the Act.

We have given these two or three examples at some length, because national systems are so many and diverse that both the universality and flexibility of ILO principles are more and more assuming world acceptance as a stabilising factor. By contrast, however, we can cite the views of the USSR delegate at the aforementioned Geneva Conference. Professor V. Kudryavtsev produced a comprehensive set of principles and stated:

> The USSR Constitution affirms and guarantees the following social and economic rights: the right to work, rest and leisure; to health protection; to social security, and to housing. In the field of culture, the Constitution guarantees the right to education, the right to the enjoyment of cultural benefits, and the right of creative freedom.

Undoubtedly, he claimed 'the constitutional rights of Soviet citizens are more extensive, socially speaking, than those written down in the basic law of many other state systems'. They include personal rights such as state protection of the family, inviolability of the person, inviolability of the home, protection of the privacy of citizens, freedom of conscience, and the right to protection by the courts. Coming to questions of 'labour discipline' and citizens' complaints, the USSR delegate insisted that 'every institution and, within the limits of his competence, every public official is obliged to respond to such approaches, to take decisions on them, and to give a reply, with the reasons therefor, within a prescribed period'.

We have, however, drawn attention in Chapter 6 to what actually happens to certain workers when they get out of line and seek to act as though these broader 'freedoms' really belonged to them as individuals. It might almost seem that the lonely individual worker is nowhere to be found in this mammoth structure of fundamental and of secondary law, even though (we quote) 'the Presidium of the Supreme Soviet is obliged to ensure observance of the Constitution of the USSR'.

The aforementioned seminar did not rest merely on reviewing the positions taken by a large number of states, but recommended that national institutions should, among other activities, collect, compile and disseminate information concerning human rights, the laws and judicial decisions relating to them and various procedures available for their promotion and protection. It urged that governments, within the framework of their constitutions, receive complaints and information directly from *any* source, individual or group, and place no restrictions on submissions of communications to and from national institutions; as well as disseminate information concerning human rights through appropriate mass communications media and press facilities. They should also publish and submit periodic reports of their activities and recommendations in the field of human rights to national authorities, including remedial or other actions secured, and, finally, 'widely publicise basic human rights texts'.

It is true that such recommendations, emanating from an authoritative United Nations Seminar in 1978, were there considered within a broader context than workers' world rights *per se*, but it can be readily agreed that: 'There is an important role in the implementation of social and economic rights for judicial tribunals, which must, where necessary, have power to issue mandatory instructions, not merely to private individuals, but also to public officials'.

The Seminar concluded that there was a strong body of opinion which believed that they would be more effective if they included specialist tribunals, exercising jurisdiction over particular fields of activity. It was felt that they should, where possible, include laymen representing the interests affected by the jurisdiction, for example labour tribunals should include representatives of the trade unions and, where they exist, of private employers. In fact, it was felt that 'provision should be made for wide and effective participation by individuals in the making of decisions, and in their practical implementation'. It was also felt that:

> Frequently this participation can best be made effective through interest-groups, which may have a role to play, not merely in making known to the authorities the views of the public, but also in providing the channel through which the authorities may communicate with the public. They may help to make the rights in question more

effective by making the public aware of them . . . The State and society must assume primary responsibility for the implementation of human rights, but wide sections of the population should participate actively in this field. Unless provision is made for satisfying this requirement, there is a danger that tensions will build up with socially undesirable results. The proper resolution of such conflicts is what human rights are about.

Notes

1. *Observer* (London, 19 November 1978).
2. UN document GE 78-8331 (1978).

APPENDICES

(Some basic texts)

A. Articles 6 to 9 of the UN Covenant on Economic, Social, and Cultural Rights
B. ILO Conventions Nos. 87 and 98
C. Text of 'Charter 77' Manifesto (Czechoslovakia)
D. Trade Union leaders executed in Chile
E. Text of Charter of 'Free Trade Union' (USSR)
F. Select Bibliography of ILO Publications

APPENDIX A

Part III of the UN Covenant on Economic, Social and Cultural Rights – Articles 6 to 9

Article 6

1. The States Parties to the present Covenant recognise the right to work, which includes the right of everyone to the opportunity to gain his living by work which he freely chooses or accepts, and will take appropriate steps to safeguard this right.
2. The steps to be taken by a State Party to the present Covenant to achieve the full realisation of this right shall include technical and vocational guidance and training programmes, policies and techniques to achieve steady economic, social and cultural development and full and productive employment under conditions safeguarding fundamental political and economic freedoms to the individual.

Article 7

The States Parties to the present Covenant recognise the right of everyone to the enjoyment of just and favourable conditions of work which ensure, in particular:
    (a) Remuneration which provides all workers, as a minimum, with:
        (i) Fair wages and equal remuneration for work of equal value without distinction of any kind, in particular women being guaranteed conditions of work not inferior to those enjoyed by men, with equal pay for equal work;
        (ii) A decent living for themselves and their families in accordance with the provisions of the present Covenant;
    (b) Safe and healthy working conditions;
    (c) Equal opportunity for everyone to be promoted in his employment to an appropriate higher level, subject to no considerations other than those of seniority and competence;
    (d) Rest, leisure and reasonable limitation of working hours and periodic holidays with pay, as well as remuneration for public holidays.

Article 8

1. The States Parties to the present Covenant undertake to ensure:

(a) The right of everyone to form trade unions and join the trade union of his choice, subject only to the rules of the organisation concerned, for the promotion and protection of his economic and social interests. No restrictions may be placed on the exercise of this right other than those prescribed by law and which are necessary in a democratic society in the interests of national security or public order or for the protection of the rights and freedoms of others;

(b) The right of trade unions to establish national federations or confederations and the right of the latter to form or join international trade-union organisations;

(c) The right of trade unions to function freely subject to no limitations other than those prescribed by law and which are necessary in a democratic society in the interests of national security or public order or for the protection of the rights and freedoms of others;

(d) The right to strike, provided that it is exercised in conformity with the laws of the particular country.

2. This article shall not prevent the imposition of lawful restrictions on the exercise of these rights by members of the armed forces or of the police or of the administration of the State.

3. Nothing in this article shall authorize States Parties to the International Labour Organisation Convention of 1948 concerning Freedom of Association and Protection of the Right to Organise to take legislative measures which would prejudice, or apply the law in such a manner as would prejudice, the guarantees provided for in that Convention.

Article 9

The States Parties to the present Covenant recognise the right of everyone to social security, including social insurance.

APPENDIX B

INTERNATIONAL LABOUR CONFERENCE

Convention 87

Convention Concerning Freedom of Association and Protection of the Right to Organise

The General Conference of the International Labour Organisation,

Having been convened at San Francisco by the Governing Body of the International Labour Office, and having met in its Thirty-first Session on 17 June 1948;

Having decided to adopt, in the form of a Convention, certain proposals concerning freedom of association and protection of the right to organise, which is the seventh item on the agenda of the session;

Considering that the Preamble to the Constitution of the International Labour Organisation declares 'recognition of the principle of freedom of association' to be a means of improving conditions of labour and of establishing peace;

Considering that the Declaration of Philadelphia reaffirms that 'freedom of expression and of association are essential to sustained progress';

Considering that the International Labour Conference, at its Thirtieth Session, unanimously adopted the principles which should form the basis for international regulation;

Considering that the General Assembly of the United Nations, at its Second Session, endorsed these principles and requested the International Labour Organisation to continue every effort in order that it may be possible to adopt one or several international Conventions;

adopts this ninth day of July of the year one thousand nine hundred and forty-eight the following Convention, which may be cited as the Freedom of Association and Protection of the Right to Organise Convention, 1948:

PART I. FREEDOM OF ASSOCIATION

Article 1

Each Member of the International Labour Organisation for which this

Convention is in force undertakes to give effect to the following provisions.

Article 2

Workers and employers, without distinction whatsoever, shall have the right to establish and, subject only to the rules of the organisation concerned, to join organisations of their own choosing without previous authorisation.

Article 3

1. Workers' and employers' organisations shall have the right to draw up their constitutions and rules, to elect their representatives in full freedom, to organise their administration and activities and to formulate their programmes.

2. The public authorities shall refrain from any interference which would restrict this right or impede the lawful exercise thereof.

Article 4

Workers' and employers' organisations shall not be liable to be dissolved or suspended by administrative authority.

Article 5

Workers' and employers' organisations shall have the right to establish and join federations and confederations and any such organisation, federation or confederation shall have the right to affiliate with international organisations of workers and employers.

Article 6

The provisions of Articles 2, 3 and 4 hereof apply to federations and confederations of workers' and employers' organisations.

Article 7

The acquisition of legal personality by workers' and employers' organisations, federations and confederations shall not be made subject to conditions of such a character as to restrict the application of the provisions of Articles 2, 3 and 4 hereof.

Article 8

1. In exercising the rights provided for in this Convention workers and employers and their respective organisations, like other persons or organised collectivities, shall respect the law of the land.

2. The law of the land shall not be such as to impair, nor shall it be so applied as to impair, the guarantees provided for in this Convention.

Article 9

1. The extent to which the guarantees provided for in this Convention shall apply to the armed forces and the police shall be determined by national laws or regulations.

2. In accordance with the principle set forth in paragraph 8 of Article 19 of the Constitution of the International Labour Organisation the ratification of this Convention by any Member shall not be deemed to affect any existing law, award, custom or agreement in virtue of which members of the armed forces or the police enjoy any right guaranteed by this Convention.

Article 10

In this Convention the term 'organisation' means any organisation of workers or of employers for furthering and defending the interests of workers or of employers.

PART II. PROTECTION OF THE RIGHT TO ORGANISE

Article 11

Each Member of the International Labour Organisation for which this Convention is in force undertakes to take all necessary and appropriate measures to ensure that workers and employers may exercise freely the right to organise.

PART III. MISCELLANEOUS PROVISIONS

Article 12

1. In respect of the territories referred to in Article 35 of the Constitution of the International Labour Organisation as amended by the Constitution of the International Labour Organisation Instrument of Amendment, 1946, other than the territories referred to in paragraphs 4 and 5 of the said Article as so amended, each Member of the Organisation which ratifies this Convention shall communicate to the Director-General of the International Labour Office with or as soon as possible after its ratification a declaration stating —

(a) the territories in respect of which it undertakes that the provisions of the Convention shall be applied without modification;

(b) the territories in respect of which it undertakes that the provi-

sions of the Convention shall be applied subject to modifications,
together with details of the said modifications;
(c) the territories in respect of which the Convention is inapplicable
and in such cases the grounds on which it is inapplicable;
(d) the territories in respect of which it reserves its decision.

2. The undertakings referred to in subparagraphs (a) and (b) of
paragraph 1 of this Article shall be deemed to be an integral part of the
ratification and shall have the force of ratification.

3. Any Member may at any time by a subsequent declaration cancel
in whole or in part any reservations made in its original declaration in
virtue of subparagraphs (b), (c) or (d) of paragraph 1 of this Article.

4. Any Member may, at any time at which this Convention is subject
to denunciation in accordance with the provisions of Article 16, communicate to the Director-General a declaration modifying in any other
respect the terms of any former declaration and stating the present
position in respect of such territories as it may specify.

Article 13

1. When the subject-matter of this Convention is within the self-
governing powers of any non-metropolitan territory, the Member responsible for the international relations of that territory may, in agreement
with the government of the territory, communicate to the Director-
General of the International Labour Office a declaration accepting on
behalf of the territory the obligations of this Convention.

2. A declaration accepting the obligations of this Convention may be
communicated to the Director-General of the International Labour
Office —
(a) by two or more Members of the Organisation in respect of any
territory which is under their joint authority; or
(b) by any international authority responsible for the administration
of any territory, in virtue of the Charter of the United Nations
or otherwise, in respect of any such territory.

3. Declarations communicated to the Director-General of the International Labour Office in accordance with the preceding paragraphs
of this Article shall indicate whether the provisions of the Convention
will be applied in the territory concerned without modification or subject to modifications; when the declaration indicates that the provisions
of the Convention will be applied subject to modifications it shall give
details of the said modifications.

4. The Member, Members or international authority concerned may
at any time by a subsequent declaration renounce in whole or in part the

right to have recourse to any modification indicated in any former declaration.

5. The Member, Members or international authority concerned may, at any time at which this Convention is subject to denunciation in accordance with the provisions of Article 16, communicate to the Director-General of the International Labour Office a declaration modifying in any other respect the terms of any former declaration and stating the present position in respect of the application of the Convention.

PART IV. FINAL PROVISIONS

Article 14

The formal ratifications of this Convention shall be communicated to the Director-General of the International Labour Office for registration.

Article 15

1. This Convention shall be binding only upon those Members of the International Labour Organisation whose ratifications have been registered with the Director-General.

2. It shall come into force twelve months after the date on which the ratifications of two Members have been registered with the Director-General.

3. Thereafter, this Convention shall come into force for any Member twelve months after the date on which its ratification has been registered.

Article 16

1. A Member which has ratified this Convention may denounce it after the expiration of ten years from the date on which the Convention first comes into force, by an act communicated to the Director-General of the International Labour Office for registration. Such denunciation shall not take effect until one year after the date on which it is registered.

2. Each Member which has ratified this Convention and which does not, within the year following the expiration of the period of ten years mentioned in the preceding paragraph, exercise the right of denunciation provided for in this Article, will be bound for another period of ten years and, thereafter, may denounce this Convention at the expiration of each period of ten years under the terms provided for in this Article.

Article 17

1. The Director-General of the International Labour Office shall

notify all Members of the International Labour Organisation of the registration of all ratifications, declarations and denunciations communicated
to him by the Members of the Organisation.

2. When notifying the Members of the Organisation of the registration of the second ratification communicated to him, the Director-
General shall draw the attention of the Members of the Organisation to
the date upon which the Convention will come into force.

Article 18

The Director-General of the International Labour Office shall communicate to the Secretary-General of the United Nations for registration in
accordance with Article 102 of the Charter of the United Nations full
particulars of all ratifications, declarations and acts of denunciation registered by him in accordance with the provisions of the preceding articles.

Article 19

At the expiration of each period of ten years after the coming into force
of this Convention, the Governing Body of the International Labour
Office shall present to the General Conference a report on the working
of this Convention and shall consider the desirability of placing on the
agenda of the Conference the question of its revision in whole or in
part.

Article 20

1. Should the Conference adopt a new Convention revising this
Convention in whole or in part, then, unless the new Convention
otherwise provides,
  (a) the ratification by a Member of the new revising Convention shall
       ipso jure involve the immediate denunciation of this Convention,
       notwithstanding the provisions of Article 16 above, if and when
       the new revising Convention shall have come into force;
  (b) as from the date when the new revising Convention comes into
       force this Convention shall cease to be open to ratification by the
       Members.

2. This Convention shall in any case remain in force in its actual form
and content for those Members which have ratified it but have not ratified
the revising Convention.

Article 21

The English and French versions of the text of this Convention are
equally authoritative.

Convention 98

Convention concerning the Application of the Principles of the Right to Organise and to Bargain Collectively

The General Conference of the International Labour Organisation,

Having been convened at Geneva by the Governing Body of the International Labour Office, and having met in its Thirty-second Session on 8 June 1949, and

Having decided upon the adoption of certain proposals concerning the application of the principles of the right to organise and to bargain collectively, which is the fourth item on the agenda of the session, and

Having determined that these proposals shall take the form of an international Convention,

adopts this first day of July of the year one thousand nine hundred and forty-nine the following Convention, which may be cited as the Right to Organise and Collective Bargaining Convention, 1949:

Article 1

1. Workers shall enjoy adequate protection against acts of anti-union discrimination in respect of their employment.

2. Such protection shall apply more particularly in respect of acts calculated to —

(a) make the employment of a worker subject to the condition that he shall not join a union or shall relinquish trade union membership;

(b) cause the dismissal of or otherwise prejudice a worker by reason of union membership or because of participation in union activities outside working hours or, with the consent of the employer, within working hours.

Article 2

1. Workers' and employers' organisations shall enjoy adequate protection against any acts of interference by each other or each other's agents or members in their establishment, functioning or administration.

2. In particular, acts which are designed to promote the establishment of workers' organisations under the domination of employers' organisations, or to support workers' organisations by financial or other means, with the object of placing such organisations under the control of employers or employers' organisations, shall be deemed to constitute acts of interference within the meaning of this Article.

Article 3

Machinery appropriate to national conditions shall be established, where necessary, for the purpose of ensuring respect for the right to organise as defined in the preceding Articles.

Article 4

Measures appropriate to national conditions shall be taken, where necessary, to encourage and promote the full development and utilisation of machinery for voluntary negotiation between employers or employers' organisations and workers' organisations, with a view to the regulation of terms and conditions of employment by means of collective agreements.

Article 5

1. The extent to which the guarantees provided for in this Convention shall apply to the armed forces and the police shall be determined by national laws or regulations.

2. In accordance with the principle set forth in paragraph 8 of article 19 of the Constitution of the International Labour Organisation the ratification of this Convention by any Member shall not be deemed to affect any existing law, award, custom or agreement in virtue of which members of the armed forces or the police enjoy any right guaranteed by this Convention.

Article 6

This Convention does not deal with the position of public servants engaged in the administration of the State, nor shall it be construed as prejudicing their rights or status in any way.

Article 7

The formal ratifications of this Convention shall be communicated to the Director-General of the International Labour Office for registration.

Article 8

1. This Convention shall be binding only upon those Members of the International Labour Organisation whose ratifications have been registered with the Director-General.

2. It shall come into force twelve months after the date on which the ratifications of two Members have been registered with the Director-General.

3. Thereafter, this Convention shall come into force for any Member

twelve months after the date on which its ratification has been registered.

Article 9

1. Declarations communicated to the Director-General of the International Labour Office in accordance with paragraph 2 of article 35 of the Constitution of the International Labour Organisation shall indicate —

  (a) the territories in respect of which the Member concerned undertakes that the provisions of the Convention shall be applied without modification;

  (b) the territories in respect of which it undertakes that the provisions of the Convention shall be applied subject to modifications, together with details of the said modifications;

  (c) the territories in respect of which the Convention is inapplicable and in such cases the grounds on which it is inapplicable;

  (d) the territories in respect of which it reserves its decision pending further consideration of the position.

2. The undertakings referred to in subparagraphs (a) and (b) of paragraph 1 of this Article shall be deemed to be an integral part of the ratification and shall have the force of ratification.

3. Any Member may at any time by a subsequent declaration cancel in whole or in part any reservation made in its original declaration in virtue of subparagraph (b), (c) or (d) of paragraph 1 of this Article.

4. Any Member may, at any time at which the Convention is subject to denunciation in accordance with the provisions of Article 11, communicate to the Director-General a declaration modifying in any other respect the terms of any former declaration and stating the present position in respect of such territories as it may specify.

Article 10

1. Declarations communicated to the Director-General of the International Labour Office in accordance with paragraph 4 or 5 of article 35 of the Constitution of the International Organisation shall indicate whether the provisions of the Convention will be applied in the territory concerned without modification or subject to modifications; when the declaration indicates that the provisions of the Convention will be applied subject to modifications, it shall give details of the said modifications.

2. The Member, Members or international authority concerned may at any time by a subsequent declaration renounce in whole or in part the right to have recourse to any modification indicated in any former declaration.

3. The Member, Members or international authority concerned may, at any time at which this Convention is subject to denunciation in accordance with the provisions of Article 11, communicate to the Director-General a declaration modifying in any other respect the terms of any former declaration and stating the present position in respect of the application of the Convention.

Article 11

1. A Member which has ratified this Convention may denounce it after the expiration of ten years from the date on which the Convention first comes into force, by an act communicated to the Director-General of the International Labour Office for registration. Such denunciation shall not take effect until one year after the date on which it is registered.
2. Each Member which has ratified this Convention and which does not, within the year following the expiration of the period of ten years mentioned in the preceding paragraph, exercise the right of denunciation provided for in this Article, will be bound for another period of ten years and, thereafter, may denounce this Convention at the expiration of each period of ten years under the terms provided for in this Article.

Article 12

1. The Director-General of the International Labour Office shall notify all Members of the International Labour Organisation of the registration of all ratifications, declarations and denunciations communicated to him by the Members of the Organisation.
2. When notifying the Members of the Organisation of the registration of the second ratification communicated to him, the Director-General shall draw the attention of the Members of the Organisation to the date upon which the Convention will come into force.

Article 13

The Director-General of the International Labour Office shall communicate to the Secretary-General of the United Nations for registration in accordance with Article 102 of the Charter of the United Nations full particulars of all ratifications, declarations and acts of denunciation registered by him in accordance with the provisions of the preceding Articles.

Article 14

At such times as it may consider necessary the Governing Body of the International Labour Office shall present to the General Conference a report on the working of this Convention and shall examine the desirability of placing on the agenda of the Conference the question of its revision in whole or in part.

Article 15

1. Should the Conference adopt a new Convention revising this Convention in whole or in part, then, unless the new Convention otherwise provides,

(a) the ratification by a Member of the new revising Convention shall *ipso jure* involve the immediate denunciation of this Convention, notwithstanding the provisions of Article 11 above, if and when the new revising Convention shall have come into force;

(b) as from the date when the new revising Convention comes into force, this Convention shall cease to be open to ratification by the Members.

2. This Convention shall in any case remain in force in its actual form and content for those Members which have ratified it but have not ratified the revising Convention.

Article 16

The English and French versions of the text of this Convention are equally authoritative.

Text of the Charter 77 Manifesto communicated by the International Confederation of Free Trade Unions by letter of 28 July 1977[1]

In the Czechoslovak Register of Laws No. 120 of 13 October 1976, texts were published of the International Covenant on Civil and Political Rights, and of the International Covenant on Economic, Social and Cultural Rights, which were signed on behalf of our Republic in 1968, reiterated at Helsinki in 1975 and came into force in our country on 23 March 1976. From that date our citizens have enjoyed the rights, and our State the duties, ensuing from them.

The human rights and freedoms underwritten by these covenants constitute features of civilised life for which many progressive movements have striven throughout history and whose codification could greatly assist humane developments in our society.

We accordingly welcome the Czechoslovak Socialist Republic's accession to those agreements.

Their publication, however, serves as a powerful reminder of the extent to which basic human rights in our country exist, regrettably, on paper alone.

The right to freedom of expression, for example, guaranteed by article 19 of the first-mentioned covenant, is in our case purely illusory. Tens of thousands of our citizens are prevented from working in their own fields for the sole reason that they hold views differing from official ones, and are discriminated against and harassed in all kinds of ways by the authorities and public organisations. Deprived as they are of any means to defend themselves, they become victims of a virtual apartheid.

Hundreds of thousands of other citizens are denied that 'freedom from fear' mentioned in the preamble to the first covenant, being condemned to the constant risk of unemployment or other penalties if they voice their own opinions.

In violation of article 13 of the second-mentioned covenant, guaranteeing everyone the right to education, countless young people are prevented from studying because of their own views or even their parents'. Innumerable citizens live in fear of their own, or their children's, right to education being withdrawn if they should ever speak up in accordance with their convictions. Any exercise of the right to 'seek, receive and impart information and ideas of all kinds, regardless of frontiers, either orally, in writing or in print' or 'in the form of art' specified in article 19, clause 2 of the first covenant is followed by extra-judicial and even judicial sanctions, often in the form of criminal charges, as in the recent trial of young musicians.

Freedom of public expression is inhibited by the centralised control of all the communication media and of publishing and cultural institutions. No philosophical, political or scientific view or artistic activity that departs ever so slightly from the narrow bounds of official ideology or aesthetics is allowed to be published; no open criticism can be made of abnormal social phenomena; no public defence is possible against false and insulting charges made in official propaganda – the legal protection against 'attacks on honour and reputation' clearly guaranteed by article 17 of the first covenant is in practice non-existent: false accusations cannot be rebutted and any attempt to secure compensation or correction through the courts is futile; no open debate is allowed in the domain of thought and art.

Many scholars, writers, artists and others are penalised for having legally published or expressed, years ago, opinions which are condemned by those who hold political power today.

Freedom of religious confession, emphatically guaranteed by article 18 of the first covenant, is continually curtailed by arbitrary official action; by interference with the activity of churchmen, who are constantly threatened by the refusal of the State to permit them the exercise of their functions, or by the withdrawal of such permission; by financial or other transactions against those who express their religious faith in word or action; by constraints on religious training and so forth.

One instrument for the curtailment or in many cases complete elimination of many civic rights is the system by which all national institutions and organisations are in effect subject to political directives from the machinery of the ruling party and to decisions made by powerful individuals.

The constitution of the Republic, its laws and legal norms do not regulate the form or content, the issuing or application of such decisions; they are often only given out verbally, unknown to the public at large and beyond its powers to check; their originators are responsible to no one but themselves and their own hierarchy; yet they have a decisive impact on the decision making and executive organs of government, justice, trade unions, interest groups and all other organisations, of the other political parties, enterprises, factories, institutions, offices and so on, for whom these instructions have precedence even before the law.

Where organisations or individuals, in the interpretation of their
rights and duties, come into conflict with such directives, they cannot
have recourse to any non-party authority, since none such exists. This
constitutes, of course, a serious limitation of the right ensuing from
articles 21 and 22 of the first-mentioned covenant, which provides for
freedom of association and forbids any restriction on its exercise, from
article 25 on the right to take part in the conduct of public affairs, and
from article 26 stipulating equal protection by the law without discrimination.

This state of affairs likewise prevents workers and others from
exercising the unrestricted right to establish trade unions and other
organisations to protect their economic and social interests, and from
freely enjoying the right to strike provided for in clause 1 of article 8
in the second-mentioned covenant.

Further civic rights, including the explicit prohibition of 'arbitrary
interference with privacy, family, home or correspondence' (article 17
of the first covenant), are seriously vitiated by the various forms of
interference in the private life of citizens exercised by the Ministry of
the Interior, for example by bugging telephones and houses, opening
mail, following personal movements, searching homes, setting up net-
works of neighbourhood informers (often recruited by illicit threats or
promises) and in other ways.

The Ministry frequently interferes in employers' decisions, instigates
acts of discrimination by authorities and organisations, brings weight to
bear on the organs of justice and even orchestrates propaganda cam-
paigns on the media. This activity is governed by no law and, being
clandestine, affords the citizen no chance to defend himself.

In cases of prosecution on political grounds the investigative and
judicial organs violate the rights of those charged and of those defending
them, as guaranteed by article 14 of the first covenant and indeed by
Czechoslovak law. The prison treatment of those sentenced in such cases
is an affront to their human dignity and a menace to their health, being
aimed at breaking their morale.

Clause 2, article 12 of the first covenant, guaranteeing every citizen
the right to leave the country, is consistently violated, or under the
pretence of 'defence of national security' is subjected to various unjustifi-
able conditions (clause 3). The granting of entry visas to foreigners is
also treated arbitrarily, and many are unable to visit Czechoslovakia merel
because of professional or personal contacts with those of our citizens
who are subject to discrimination.

Some of our people – either in private, at their places of work or by
the only feasible public channel, the foreign media – have drawn attention to the systematic violation of human rights and democratic freedoms and demanded amends in specific cases. But their pleas have
remained largely ignored or been made grounds for police investigation.

Responsibility for the maintenance of civic rights in our country
naturally devolves in the first place on the political and state authorities.
Yet not only on them: everyone bears his share of responsibility for the
conditions that prevail and accordingly also for the observance of legally
enshrined agreements, binding upon all individuals as well as upon
governments.

It is this sense of co-responsibility, our belief in the importance of its
conscious public acceptance and the general need to give it new and
more effective expression that led us to the idea of creating Charter 77,
whose inception we today publicly announce.

Charter 77 is a loose, informal and open association of people of
various shades of opinion, faiths and professions united by the will to
strive individually and collectively for the respecting of civic and human
rights in our own country and throughout the world – rights accorded
to all men by the two mentioned international covenants, by the Final
Act of the Helsinki Conference and by numerous other international
documents opposing war, violence and social or spiritual oppression, and
which are comprehensively laid down in the UN Universal Charter of
Human Rights.

Charter 77 springs from a background of friendship and solidarity
among people who share our concern for those ideals that have inspired,
and continue to inspire, their lives and their work.

Charter 77 is not an organisation; it has no rules, permanent bodies
or formal membership. It embraces everyone who agrees with its ideas
and participates in its work. It does not form the basis for any opposi-
tional political activity. Like many similar citizen initiatives in various
countries, West and East, it seeks to promote the general public interest.

It does not aim, then, to set out its own platform of political or
social reform or change, but within its own field of impact to conduct a
constructive dialogue with the political and state authorities, particularly
by drawing attention to individual cases where human and civic rights
are violated, to document such grievances and suggest remedies, to make
proposals of a more general character calculated to reinforce such rights
and machinery for protecting them, to act as intermediary in situations
of conflict which may lead to violation of rights, and so forth.

By its symbolic name Charter 77 denotes that it has come into being at the start of a year proclaimed as Political Prisoners Year – a year in which a conference in Belgrade is due to review the implementation of the obligations assumed at Helsinki.

As signatories, we hereby authorise Professor Dr. Jan Patocka, Dr. Vaclav Havel and Professor Dr. Jiri Hajek to act as the spokesmen for the Charter. These spokesmen are endued with full authority to represent it vis-à-vis state and other bodies, and the public at home and abroad, and their signatures attest the authenticity of documents issued by the Charter. They will have us and others who join us as their colleagues, taking part in any needful negotiations, shouldering particular tasks and sharing every responsibility.

We believe that Charter 77 will help to enable all the citizens of Czechoslovakia to work and live as free human beings.

Prague, 1 January 1977.   (Signatures of 257 Czechoslovak citizens.)

Note

1. Reproduced from ILO document GB 206/5/8 (2 June 1978).

APPENDIX D

Trade Union Leaders or Former Leaders About Whom the Commission Requested Information from the Chilean Government[1]

A. Leaders or former leaders who, according to the complaining organisations, were killed or executed

1. According to the Government (or other sources indicated) the following were executed:

ARANEDA, Vladimir, a former miners' trade union leader; according to the Government, he was not a union leader. Executed on 22 October 1973 after sentencing by court-martial at Concepción.

ARQUEROS, Mario, former secretary of the saltpetre workers' union. Prosecuted in Case No. 6-73 (military authorities, Antofagasta) and executed on 18 October 1973.

BARRIENTOS, Werner José, CUT youth leader, Valdivia. Tried in Valdivia (Case No. 1323), condemned to death by court-martial on 2 October 1973, and executed.

CABRERA, Bernabé, a leader of the Lota coalminers' union. According to the Government, there is no record of his having been a trade union leader. Executed on 22 October 1973 after being condemned by court-martial in Concepción.

CARRILLO, Isidoro, a former miners' leader, director of the Lota mining company. General manager of the National Coal Company, court-martialled at Concepción and executed on 22 October 1973.

GARCIA, Ricardo, a trade unionist, and former head of the CUT technical department. According to the Government, this must be Ricardo Hugo García Posada. Prosecuted (Case No. 385-73) by the military authorities at El Salvador and executed.

LIENDO, José Gregorio, secretary of the Panguipulli Peasants' Union. According to the Government, was an extremist known as Commander Pepe, in command of an armed band. Prosecuted by the Valdivia military authorities for breach of Act No. 17,798 (section 8), condemned to death by court-martial on 2 October 1973 and executed.

MIRANDA, David, former general secretary of the Miners' Federation. The information submitted by the Government relates to somebody of the same name, under arrest in Ritoque. A member of the family con-

165

firmed that Miranda, industrial relations manager at the Chuquicamata Copper Mine, a former FINM leader, was shot in Calama on 19 October 1973.

RUZ DIAZ, Juan, a customs-officers' trade union leader at Iquique. Prosecuted by the local military authorities as one of the top men in the AGP movement which was preparing an armed rising and an attack on the armed forces. Sentenced by court-martial on 29 October 1973 and executed on 30 October 1973.

TAPIA, Benito, a leader of the El Salvador industrial union (copper mines). Sentenced by the Copiapó military prosecutor and executed.

VALENZUELA FLORES, Alexis, a leader of the CUT at Tocopilla. Indicted by the local military prosecutor and executed in accordance with the sentence passed.

2. *According to the Government, the following were killed in clashes with the armed forces:*

ALMONACID ARELLANO, Luis, general secretary of the O'Higgins CUT provincial office. Killed at Rancagua on 11 September 1973.

COSSIO, Moisés, a peasants' leader in the Lampa area. Killed on 25 September 1973.

CHAMORRO, Hernán, a railway trade unionist, but not, according to the Government, a trade union leader. Killed in October 1973.

GONZALEZ MAUREIRA, Servando, chairman of the Rayon Sahid industrial union. Killed in Santiago on 25 September 1973.

MARTINEZ, Juan, former national leader of the leather and footwear workers' union. Killed in October 1973.

MONSALVE, Ariel, a railway trade unionist.

RODRIGUEZ, José Eusebio, secretary in San Antonio. According to the Government, was not recorded as being a trade union leader. An agitator and an extremist, killed in a clash with the armed forces on 14 September 1973.

SALAZAR, Teobaldo, leader of teaching staff and employees at the University of Chile, Santiago. Killed in October 1973.

VIVANCO, Ramón, a railway trade unionist.

3. *According to the Government, the following died in attempts to escape, or in similar circumstances:*

ALVAREZ, Guillermo; JIMENEZ, Armando; NUÑEZ, Samuel; ROJO, Hector; maritime workers' leaders, San Antonio. Killed on 22 September 1973, when armed extremists attacked the vehicle in which they were travelling.

BACCIARINI ZORRILLA, Raúl Enrique, a port workers' leader, San Antonio. Killed on 24 September 1972 while attempting to escape.
BRAVO AVLAREZ, Fidel, a port workers' leader, San Antonio. Killed on 24 September 1973, while attempting to escape.
DONOSO, Manuel, a leader of the Arica school-teachers. Mortally injured in a motor accident during his transfer to Pisagua.
ELGUETA, Gaston, secretary, National Health Service, Temuco. Arrested for a breach of the Weapons Control Act. Killed on 25 November 1973, when attempting to escape from the Tucapel Regimental Barracks. Not a trade union leader.
FLORRES PEREZ, Alejandro, CUT director of trade union affairs, Cautín. Detained for breaches of the State Security Act in the Tucapel Barracks; killed on 2 October 1973 while attempting to escape.
GUZMAN, Marcelo, trade union secretary, National Health Service. Shot on 3 November 1973, attempting to escape from Pisagua.
JARA RIOS, Eliseo, a trade union leader, Victoria. On 27 October 1973, while events were being reconstructed by the authorities at the California Ranch, he tried to escape and lost his life.
MATELUNA GOMEZ, Daniel, a CUT leader, Temuco. Detained, for a breach of the Weapons Control Act, in the Tucapel Barracks, and killed on 2 October 1973 when attempting to escape.
NEHEGMAN, Lecar, secretary of the National Health Service, Temuco. According to the Government, not registered as a trade union leader. Arrested for a breach of the Weapons Control Act and killed on 25 November 1973 while trying to escape from the Tucapel Barracks, where he was held awaiting trial.

4. According to the Government, the following have been sentenced, detained or exiled:

BARROS, Eduardo, former CUT secretary, San Antonio. Sentenced in Case No. 40-73, military prosecutor there, for a breach of Act 12,927, and now exiled to San Fernando for three years.
CORDOVA, José, a port workers' leader, Iquique. According to the Government, this must be José Córdova Cancino, an 'anti-social element' held at the Iquique penitentiary.
CORNEJO FAUNDEZ, Pedro, national secretary of the Peasants' Union. Detained but appears in the list of those who will be released by virtue of certain conventions (International Red Cross, International Committee for European Migration, COMAR).
GORDILLO HITSCHFELD, Iván, a CUT leader, Antofagasta Province. In Case No. 20-73, heard by the First Military Court at Antofagasta, was

sentenced to twenty years' imprisonment for a breach of the State Security Act. Now in Antofagasta prison.

LOBOS, Edgar, a school-teachers' leader, San Felipe. Sentenced to three years' exile for breach of the State Security Act. Serving his sentence in San Felipe.

MADARIAGA, Luis, leader of the Colchague peasants' committee. Chairman of the El Surco Federation of Agricultural Unions. Held in San Fernando prison by virtue of Act 12,927.

MARTINEZ MOLINA, Héctor, a peasants' leader. Being prosecuted by the Second Military Prosecutor, Santiago.

MORAGA, Ethiel, a leader of the Sewells (El Teniente) industrial union. Being held at Ritoque, awaiting trial.

ORELLANA ABARCA, Manuel Jesus, a CUT leader at San Francisco de Mostazal. Condemned to five years' imprisonment for a breach of Act No. 17,798; held in Rancagua prison.

TELLO, Osvaldo, chairman of the Chuquicamata industrial union. Sentenced to 500 days' imprisonment (Case 21-73) by the military court at Calama.

VARGAS, Arturo, chairman of the industrial union at the Maria Elena Saltpetre Pans. According to the Government, this must be the chairman of the SOQUIMICH union, sentenced to three years' exile by the Antofagasta military court. Serving his sentence in Salamanca.

5. According to the Government, the following are at liberty:

AGUILA, Onofre, national secretary, Retired Seamen's Union. On 10 October 1974, freely left the country for Argentina.

AVILA VELAZQUEZ, Juan, a peasants' leader of the Panguipulli forestry complex. Arrested on 19 September 1973 for presumed participation in an armed attack on the police at Neltume. Released by virtue of a stay of judgment on 11 October 1973.

BADILLA, Ambrosio, a peasants' leader, Cautín. According to the Government, this must be the Ambrosio Badilla Vasey who in September 1973 freely travelled to Argentina.

CORTES MONROY, Marcial, a leader of the Chilean Private Employees' Federation.

GARAY, Samuel, a trade union secretary in Valdivia.

MASARELLO, Vitalio, chairman of the miners' union at San Pedro de Atacama.

MORAGA, Orlando, leader of the Caletones industrial union (El Teniente). Seems to have left for Italy in October 1974.

OYARZUN, Pedro, a railway trade unionist. At liberty in Puerto Montt.

RIFFO, Juan, chairman of FENATS, tenth health area.

ROJAS, Luis, general secretary of the CUT, Arica area.

SANTANA, Raúl, leader of the CUT provincial council in Osorno.

TORRES GOMEZ, Carlos R., a CUT leader, Cautín Province.

VALENZUELA, Juan, a leader of the industrial union at the Pedro de Valdivia saltpetre works.

6. According to the Government, there is no record of the following having been detained or executed:

ACEVEDO, Alfredo, a railwaymen's trade unionist.

AILIO, José, a peasant leader, Cautín Province.

ALARCON, secretary of the Pedro Léon Gallo agricultural workers' union.

ALVAREZ, Santiago, a CUT leader, Coquimbo Province.

ALVEAR, Luis, CUT trade union secretary, Coquimbo Province.

ASTORGA, Fredy, secretary, CUT youth section.

AVILA, César, provincial leader, Osorno teachers' union.

BARRIA, Pedro, CUT youth leader, Valdivia.

BASTIAS, Juan, a CUT leader, Temuco. According to the Government, this must be the Julián Bastias Rebolledo who has sought asylum in the Netherlands Embassy.

BURGOS, Anibal, activist from Lautaro. The Government presumes that he is in Argentina.

CALABRAN, Claudio, provincial leader of the education workers.

CARRASCO, Pedro, a peasants' leader from Alicahue.

CARREÑO, Alfonso, a CUT leader, Ñuñoa area.

CARREÑO, Ramón, a CUT youth leader, Cautín.

CARVEÑO, Ramón, youth secretary.

CASTILLO, Hernán, a leader of the telephone employees.

CHAVES, Juan, a student leader and CUT secretary in Cautín (youth section).

CIAVIDO, Orlando, chairman of the fishermen's unions.

DIAZ, Sergio, CUT general secretary, Iquique Province.

ESPINOZA, Patricio, a SUTE leader, Lota.

FLORES, Belson, an INDAP unionist.

HADD, Julio, trade union secretary, Cautín-Lautaro.

HUANANTE ROCHA, Francisco, trade union relations officer, Valparaiso.

HUENTELAF, Félix, a CUT leader, Cautín Province.

LOPEZ, Leopoldo, a leader of the fair and market salesmen.

MAMANI, Luis, a leader of the public employees, Calama.

MAUREIRA, Sergio, a peasants' leader, Maipo Island.
MELLADO, Juan, a peasants' leader from Santa Bárbara. The Government refers to a 'Juan Bautista Mellado'.
MONTECINOS, Carlos, general secretary, Peasants' Provincial Council, Coihueco, Ñuble Province.
MUÑOZ, Omar, a CUT leader, Coquimbo Province.
NAHUELCOI (brothers), peasant leaders, Cautín Province.
NORAMBUERA, Luis, CUT general Secretary, San Antonio Area.
PINTO VIEL, Guillermo, formerly a trade union secretary.
PURRAN, Guillermo, a Mapuche peasant leader, Santa Bárbara.
RAMIREZ DEL PRADO, Robinson, CUT general secretary, Ñuble Province.
RODRIGUEZ, Alejandro, former chairman of the Copper Workers' Confederation.
SANTIS, Ceferino, a CUT leader and national textile-workers' leader.
SEREGA, Victor, a trade unionist and a member of the CUT executive committee.
SOBARZO, Javier, a trade union delegate in Santiago.
URRUTIA ACEVEDO, Cleofe, a leader of the Chillán Taxi-Drivers' Union.
VALDIVIA, Luis, a leader of the Calama public employees. According to the Government, this might well be the Luis Valdivia Carrasco, who in 1944 was chairman of the Calama bakers' union.
VIDAL, Alex, a member of the Valdivia regional council.
VILLALOBOS, C., chairman of the Chuquicamata Voluntary Action Committee. This man, according to the Government, must be Carlos Villalobos.
VILLALOBOS, Luis, former trade union leader of the Chuquicamata clerical workers.
VAÑEZ, Manuel, a port workers' leader. The Government says that it has no record of his being a trade union leader.

7. According to the Government, it has been impossible to trace the following from the data supplied:

AVILA MARQUEZ, Roberto, a railway trade unionist.
CASTO, Raúl, a railway trade unionist.
COFREDES, Arturo, a railway trade unionist.
FARIAS (brothers), leaders of the 'Pesquera de Chile' union, San Antonio. Not recorded as among the San Antonio fishermen's trade union leaders.
GONZALEZ, Manuel, a railway trade unionist.

MORALES, José, railway trade union leader, San Bernardo Arsenal.

MORILLO, José, a railway trade unionist.

SILVA, José, a railway trade unionist.

8. With regard to FERNANDEZ, Jorge, the CERA peasants' leader at Nehuentue, the Government says that he was not a trade union leader but a student, and died before 10 September 1973, in a clash among civilians, while he was carrying grenades with a view to taking over a farm in Nehuentue.

B. Leaders or former leaders stated by the complainant organisations to have been detained

1. *According to the Government, one of the persons detained was killed.*

JIMENEZ, Juan, a leader of the CORFO workers' association, killed on 3 October 1973, when trying to escape from Pisagua.

2. *According to the Government, the following were sentenced to imprisonment:*

ALARCON, Francisco, CUT general vice-secretary, Magallanes Province. A political agitator, according to the Government. Prosecuted by the naval authorities Punta Arenas (Case 23-73) and condemned to twelve years' penal servitude, which he is serving in La Serena prison.

CIFUENTES TORRES, José Luis, CUT general secretary, Bío-Bío Province. Prosecuted in Los Angeles for a breach of Acts 12,927 and 17,798, and sentenced to five years' penal servitude. His name has been put forward for emigration.

CONTRERAS, Luis, CUT organisational secretary, Talca Province. Held on 11 September 1973 for having played a part in a commando raid by extremists on police stores, and sentenced to life imprisonment, which he is now serving in Talca. Accused of assaulting the police, causing death; theft of war material, and breach of the Weapons Control Act.

LARA, Adolfo, former leader of the Sewells industrial union, El Teniente. Prosecuted by the O'Higgins military authorities for a breach of Act 17,798, and sentenced to five years' penal servitude. Is in Rancagua prison.

LEE, Miguel Angel, a leader of the Copper Workers' Confederation. Prosecuted by the Rancagua military authorities. (According to other information received by the Commission, was sentenced to nine years and six months' imprisonment.)

MARIÑO, Luis, a leader of the Machalí municipal employees' union, now serving a five-year sentence in Rancagua for a breach of Act 17,798.

MONDACA GALVEZ, Daniel, former leader of the Santiago combined union of the El Teniente Mining Co. Prosecuted by the O'Higgins military authorities for breaches of Acts 12,927 and 17,798, and is now serving a three-year sentence in Rancagua prison. (According to additional information obtained by the Commission, he was thereafter sentenced to a further 11 years for another crime, both sentences are to run concurrently.)
SOTO, Jorge, a FENATS leader from Osorno. Prosecuted (Case No. 151-73) by the Osorno military authorities for a breach of Act 17,798, and now serving a five-year sentence in Osorno prison.

3. According to the Government, the following are detained, exiled or under house arrest:

ALEMANY GONZALEZ, Claudio, teacher and SUTE activist. Detained at Puchuncaví under Act 12,927. Appears in a list of persons whose exit from Chile is being negotiated.
ALARCON, Alejandro, a textile workers' leader and former CUT national official. Detained in Puchuncaví. Name appears among those of persons who may be leaving the country.
ARAYA, Lorenzo, CUT general secretary, Antofagasta. Prosecuted for a breach of Act 12,927 and sentenced to three years' exile in Mulchén.
AROS, Jaime, leader of an industrial union, El Teniente. Transferred to Limache and under house arrest.
ARREDONDO, Luis, direct of a clerical workers' union, El Teniente. Transferred to Chillán and under house arrest.
BRAVO, Juan Bautista, CUT provincial secretary, Concepción. Held at Puchuncaví for a breach of Act 12,927.
BARRAZA, Juana, a trade union leader from the Social Development Corporation, a body about which the Government disclaims any knowledge. This may be the woman known as Juana Enriqueta Barraza Celada, tried on 3 October 1974 and held in San Antonio.
CAVIESES, Manuel, chairman of the 'Ultima Hora' workers' union. Held at Puchuncaví, and appears in the list of persons about whose exit from Chile negotiations are proceeding.
CERECEDA, Lautaro, chairman of the National Association of Tax Employees. Held at Puchuncaví, and appears in the list of those about whose exit from Chile negotiations are proceeding.
CISTERÑAS PEÑA, Emilio, a leader of the Concepción CUT provincial branch. Held in Puchuncavi pending trial.
CORNEJO FAUNDEZ, Pedro, a CUT national leader. Held at Tres Alamos, Santiago (mentioned already in Part A).

CURA, Antonio, a leader of the Rengo Commercial Travellers' Union. Now in San Vicente de Tagua-Tagua, under house arrest.

GACITUA, Yolanda, a Copiapó health workers' leader, held for a breach of Act 12,927. She has been exiled to Vallemar.

GAJARDO, Germán, undersecretary, CUT Chillán. Was in Chillán, under military supervision, up to 31 December 1974.

GONZALEZ, Juan Elpidio, a leader of the national seamen's association. Held in Chin-Chin prison.

GONZALEZ, Mario, a copper workers' trade union leader, Chuquicamata. Exiled to southern Chile.

GUERRERO, José, a leader of the Machalí municipal employees' union. Under house arrest.

GUTIERREZ, Luisa, a leader of the Machali municipal employees' union. She is now in Chillán, under house arrest. Has been authorised to leave the country.

GUZMAN ORDENES, Alamiro, chairman of the National Mining Industry Federation. Held at Ritoque for a breach of Act 12,927.

HERRERA, Juan, chairman of the Bernardo O'Higgins Peasants' Federation. The Government supplied information about one Juan Francisco Herrera Cabrera, tried for a breach of Act 17,798, whose appeal for permission to leave the country was granted, and about a certain Juan Herrera Sánchez, treasurer of the Martínez de Rozas agricultural workers' union, whose name does not appear among those detained or executed.

IBARRA, Luis, former leader of the Caletones union, El Teniente. Has not been registered as a trade union official for the last eight years. Transferred to Vallemar and under house arrest.

KRUHN, Heriberto, CUT organisational secretary, Concepción. Held at Puchuncaví, and appears in the list of those about whose exit from Chile negotiations are proceeding.

LIBERONA, Victor, a leader of the Copper Workers' Confederation. Subject to house arrest in Tocopilla.

LOPEZ, Patricio, a textile worker, supervisor of the textile workers' federation at Tomé and Santiago. Arrested in Concepción on 3 October 1974.

MADARIAGA, José, chairman of the El Surco peasants' federation, Colchagua. Held in San Fernando prison under Act 12,927.

MARDONES, Guillermo, a Cholguán trade union leader. Held in Chillán, and prosecuted by the Ñuble military authorities.

MARIN, Manuel, chairman of the Coya-Pangal union, El Teniente. Transferred to Collipulli under house arrest.

MONTES, Jorge, former leader of the Chilean Teachers' Union. The Government says that he had been a member of parliament since 1957 and a senator since 1969. Held at Ritoque.

MORALES, Polidoro, a CUT national leader. Held at the disposal (Case No. 8-74) of the Air Force Prosecutor.

NAVARRO, Mario, a former WFTU secretary and CUT national councillor. Detained at Ritoque by virtue of the state of emergency.

NAZAR, Jacinto, of the Ranquil National Peasants' Confederation. Does not appear to be registered as a trade union official. Held at Ritoque by virtue of Act 12,927.

OÑATE, Rolando, a trade union leader, Cholguán. Held in Yungay prison, prosecuted by the Ñuble military authorities.

PEIFORD, Isabel, secretary of the fishermen's union. Imprisoned at Pisagua.

QUINTANA, Juan, former leader of the Copper Workers' Confederation. Held at Rancagua.

RODRIGUEZ, Arnaldo, a SUTE trade union leader, Teno. Held in Curicó by virtue of the state of emergency.

RODRIGUEZ MOYA, Edmundo, a former national leader of the leather and footwear workers' union. Prosecuted under Case No. 197-74.

SALINAS MONTECINOS, a peasants' trade union leader, Teno. Held at Ritoque.

ULLOA, Armando, CUT general secretary for the Province of Magallanes. Held at the disposal of the Punta Arenas military court (Case No. 21-73).

VALDES, Juvenal, a former leader of the Lota miners' union. Held at Tres Alamos under Act 12,927.

VASQUEZ, Rolando, a CUT national leader. Exiled to the south.

VENEGAS, Hernán, a CUT leader, Ñuble. In Chillán prison under Act 12,927.

ZULJEVIC LOVRIN, Leopoldo, a Valparaiso trade union leader and former superintendent of customs. Held at Ritoque by virtue of the state of emergency.

4. *According to the Government, the following are at liberty:*

AGUILERA, María, leader at the El Salvador Hospital.

AREVALO, María, a peasants' trade union leader, Arauco.

BRAVO, Heriberto, CUT leader for the Quillota area. Left Chile of his own free will on 28 February 1974 for Buenos Aires.

BRAVO, María, a leader of the workers' association at the University of Chile.

CARRASCO, Luis, an ASMAR trade union leader, Talcahuano.

CONTRERAS, Arturo, a leader of the Steel Workers' Federation, Talcahuano.

CONTRERAS, Omar, secretary, Port Workers' Federation.

CUADRA SALDIAS, Brunilda, secretary of the fishermen's union, prosecuted by the Iquique military authorities. Exiled for six months to Linares.

CHANDIA, Rosa, a leader of the El As factory union.

DIAZ, Mario, CUT secretary, Iquique.

ESPINOSA, Leoncio, an EQUITERM union leader, Talcahuano.

EYZAGUIRRE, Alberto, director of the Association of Employees of the Sindicatura de Quiebras (Bankruptcy Office). At present in Sweden.

GONZALEZ, Abel, chairman of the INACAP single union.

GONZALEZ, Mario, chairman of the Hirmas textile mill union.

GONZALEZ, Salatiel, a SUTE leader at Rancagua.

GODOY, Evaristo, a miner from Cabildo, Aconcagua, founder of the Independent Miners' Federation. Granted a stay of proceedings for breach of the State Security and Weapons Control Acts.

GUTIERREZ, Luis, former CUT vice-secretary, Ñuble. Granted a stay of proceedings in Case No. 36-73, brought by the Ñuble military prosecutor.

GUZMAN, Luis, a leader of the Copper Workers' Confederation. According to the Government, in 1969 held office in that Confederation. Now works in Valparaiso, in the El Teniente Mining Co.

HAUSTEINS, Enrique, a worker, chairman of the Schwager Coal Miners' Federation; a former Governor of Coronel.

HERRERA, Herminio, a leader of the Ranquil Peasants' Confederation.

IBAÑEZ, Oscar, former CUT national leader.

LINEO, Laura, Arica health workers' leader.

MICHILLANCA, Hoel, a leader of the Valdivia regional fishermen's federation.

MONTECINOS ACEVEDO, Alfredo, chairman of the Chilean Maritime Confederation. At present not occupying this post. Now head of the Stevedores' Union, Antofagasta, in which city he normally works.

MONTOYA, Estanislao, a SUTE leader in Concepción.

MUÑOZ, Hernán, CUT leader, Melipilla area.

NUÑEZ, Pedro, former chairman of the INACAP single union.

OJEDA, Juan, national leader of the health workers.

OLIVEROS, Manuel, head of the CUT provincial council, Linares. Acquitted in Case No. 12-73.

PEZOA, Marcos, a leader of the El Teniente industrial mining union. According to the Government, in 1971 held office in the Braden Copper industrial union. Not at present an officer.

RIQUELME, Sara, a leader of the Hoescht Chemical Workers' Union. The Government says that she does not appear as a trade union official in this concern. The woman in question must be Sara Riquelme Fuentes, who is at liberty.

ROJAS, Glasfira, union official, Clinic No. 5, Santiago.

SANCHEZ, Iván, CUT general secretary, Osorno Province. At present at liberty in Entre Lagos.

SANHUEZA, Omar, chairman of a union at Lota.

TORRES, Orlando, chairman of the Luchetti industrial union.

VENEGAS ZAMORA, Datan, a leader of the National Customs Officers' Association.

VILLALOBOS, Sergio, chairman of the Ranquil Peasants' Confederation.

VILLENA, Luis, a leader of the Copper Workers' Confederation.

ZAMORA, Germán, a leader of the Melipilla health workers. On 11 August 1974, left for Frankfurt.

ZAMORANO, Adolfo, a FENATS leader.

5. *According to the Government, there is no record of the following having been detained or executed:*

ACEVEDO, Juan, leader of a peasants' union, Machalí.

ALARCON, Eliseo, leader, building workers' union.

ARAVENA, Edelmiro, national leader, building workers.

AVILES, Enrique, trade union leader, Cholguán.

CASTILLO, Manuel, secretary to the Transport Workers' Union.

CRUCES, Armando, a leader of the Elecmetal Union. On 3 November 1973, left the firm of Electro-Metalúrgica, S.A.

ECHEVERRIA, Roberto, chairman of the Federation of Agricultural and Forestry Workers.

GONZALEZ, Filadelfia, union official, Clinic No. 5, Santiago.

GONZALEZ, Isidoro, SUTE chairman, Concepción.

IRRAZABAL, Luis, leader of the peasants' union, Machalí.

LARA, Osvaldo, national leader, Building Workers' Union.

MACIA, Anselmo, a leader of the Electricians' Federation, Puerto Montt.

MILLAPE, Antonio, chairman of the Mapuche National Peasants' Confederation.

OJEDA, Sonia, a health workers' leader, Chillán.

PAINE, Domingo, an employees' leader, Rural Educational Institute.

PALAVICINO, Luis, a SUTE leader in Rancagua.

PEDREROS, Robinson, a worker, supervisor in the union of the Canteras Lonco Company, Concepción.

PEREZ, José, a leader of the Ralco union, Concepción.

POLANCO, David, a CUT national leader.

POVEDA, Simon, a trade union leader, Cholguán.

URIBE, Yolanda, a health workers' leader, Concepción.

Note

1. The information about the trade union duties performed has been supplied by the complainants.

Charter of the Free Trade Union (USSR)

Among the documents smuggled to the West by dissident Soviet workers earlier this year was the Charter below, establishing and outlining the program of the unofficial Free Trade Union Association of Workers in the Soviet Union. The document was published for the first time in the West in the May AFL-CIO *Free Trade Union News*, (1978).

Charter

of the Free Trade Union Association of workers in the Soviet Union. Effective from 1 January, 1978 to 1 January, 1979.

Part One. Membership of the Free Trade Union Association of Workers in the Soviet Union

1. Membership in the Free Trade Union Association is open to any worker or employee whose rights and interests have been unlawfully violated by administrative, governmental, Party or judicial agencies.

2. A member of the Free Trade Union Association has the right to:

    a. discuss freely all of the activities of the Association, make suggestions and openly express and defend his opinions prior to the Free Trade Union Association's coming to any decision;

    b. personally take part in meetings which pertain to his own activities or behaviour;

    c. conduct a ceaseless battle for peace and friendship among peoples;

    d. raise the level of political consciousness;

    e. uphold the Charter of the Free Trade Union Association;

    f. carry out the social obligations with which he is charged by the association.

3. A member of the Association has the following advantages:

    a. he receives proper legal counsel;

    b. he receives moral and material assistance from the Association to the extent to which it is available;

    c. he receives help in finding living accommodations, if such assistance is available, and helps his colleagues.

4. Membership in the Free Trade Union Association is based on the individual's personal desire to join, with one week's time given for contemplation, because of the possible consequences which may ensue as a result of his joining the Association.

5. Decisions regarding the acceptance of new members are made during Association meetings.

Part Two. Organisational Structure of the Free Trade Union Association of Workers

6. It is based on the principle of democratic centralism, which means:

    a. everyone from the lower to the upper ranks is elected by the members of the Association and is accountable to them;

    b. all questions concerning the Association are decided in accordance with the Charter;

    c. decisions are made by majority vote.

7. A free and businesslike discussion of questions concerning the Trade Union Association is an important principle of internal trade union democracy. Concepts of criticism and self-criticism, the activities and the initiative of Association members develop on the basis of this principle, and the level of consciousness and business discipline are strengthened by it.

8. The Free Trade Union Association is based on the association initially formed by the 'forty-three' members.

9. The purposes of the Free Trade Union Association are:

    a. to carry out the obligations reached by collective bargaining;

    b. to induce workers and other employees into joining free trade union associations;

    c. to carry out those decisions of the Association which concern the defense of rights and the seeking of justice;

    d. to educate Association members in the spirit of irreconcilability toward deficiencies, bureaucracy, deception, inefficiency and wastefulness, and a negligent attitude to national health.

Part Three. Means of Support of the Association of the Free Trade Union

10. The Free Trade Union Association will depend on the following means of support:

    a. monthly membership dues and on contributions of unemployed members made within their means;

    b. dues which will comprise not over one per cent of the working members' salaries and on unlimited voluntary contributions;

    c. fees paid by non-members for legal services, the preparation and typing of complaints, etc. but the fees shall not exceed state tariffs;

    d. material aid received from foreign professional trade union organisations.

Part Four. The Rights of the Free Trade Union Association as a Legal
Entity

11. The Free Union Association [sic] of workers in the Soviet Union is
a legal entity.

As soon as the Free Trade Union Association of workers in the Soviet
Union will be recognised by the International Labour Organisation or
by professional trade unions of foreign countries, and after it will have
received moral and material support, it will review its Charter, keeping
in mind the specific conditions of workers in our country. Such a review
will be conducted not earlier than one year after the Association's
founding.

Council of the 'forty-three' members of
the Free Trade Union of workers
in the Soviet Union

Moscow   February 1, 1978

[The Charter is signed by 110 persons, with a note stating that 'theie
are a number of other colleagues who have asked that for the time being
their names be withheld.']

APPENDIX F

Select Bibliography of ILO Publications Concerning Human Rights
(to January 1979)

General

Constitution of the International Labour Organisation. November 1977
edition, 87 pp.

THE ILO and Human Rights. Report of the Director-General (Part 1)
to the International Labour Conference, 52nd Session, Geneva, 1968;
report presented by the International Labour Organisation to the
International Conference on Human Rights, 1968, 118 pp.

*Freedom by Dialogue: Economic Development by Social Progress: The
ILO Contribution.* Report of the Director-General, Part 1, International
Labour Conference, 56th Session, Geneva 1971, 54 pp.

Poverty and Minimum Living Standards: The Role of the ILO. Report
of the Director-General, Part 1, International Labour Conference,
54th Session, Geneva, 1970, 122 pp.

*Technology for Freedom – Man in his Environment: the ILO Contri-
bution.* Report of the Director-General, Part 1, International Labour
Conference, 57th Session, Geneva, 1972, 58 pp.

*Prosperity for Welfare – Social Purpose In Economic Growth and
Change: the ILO Contribution.* Report of the Director-General, Part 1,
International Labour Conference, 58th Session, Geneva, 1973, 63 pp.

Action of the ILO, Problems and Prospects. Report of the Director-
General, International Labour Conference, 59th Session, Geneva,
1974, 91 pp.

*Conventions and Recommendations Adopted by the International
Labour Conference, 1919-66.* xvi, 1176 pp. (Conventions and
Recommendations adopted since 1966 may be found in the ILO
Official Bulletin; they are also available as separate leaflets.)

The International Labour Code, 1951. A systematic arrangement of the
Conventions and Recommendations adopted by the International
Labour Conference, 1919-51, with appendices embodying other standards of social policy framed by or with the cooperation of the International Labour Organisation, 1919-51. 1952, 2 vols.

*Reports of the Committee of Experts on the Application of Conven-
tions and Recommendations.* General report and observations con-

cerning particular countries. Submitted each year to the International
Labour Conferences as Report III (Part 4A).

*Reports of the Committee on the Application of Conventions and
Recommendations.* International Labour Conference, Third item on
the agenda: Information and reports on the application of Conventions and Recommendations. Offprints from the records of proceedings of each general session of the Conference.

International Labour Standards. Public information booklet, 1978,
48 pp.

Chart of Ratifications. Published as of 1 January each year.

The Impact of International Labour Conventions and Recommendations,
1976, vi, 104 pp.

International Labour Standards: A Workers' Education Manual. 1978,
vi, 98 pp.

Valticos N., 'Fifty Years of Standard-setting Activities by the International
Labour Organisation.' *International Labour Review,* September 1969,
pp. 201-237.

Landy, E.A., 'The Influence of International Labour Standards: Possibilities and Performance.' *International Labour Review,* June 1970,
pp. 555-604.

'Comparative Analaysis of the International Covenants on Human Rights
and International Labour Conventions and Recommendations.'
Official Bulletin, 1969, No. 2, pp. 181-216.

*Report by the Committee of Experts on the Application of Conventions
and Recommendations of the International Labour Organisation on
Progress in Achieving Observance of the Provisions of Articles 6 to 9
of the International Covenant on Economic, Social and Cultural
Rights.* 71 pp. (UN E/1978/27, 6 April, 1978).

Trade Union Rights

*ILO Principles, Standards and Procedures Concerning Freedom of
Association.* 1978, 25 pp.

*Freedom of Association and Collective Bargaining: General Survey on
the Reports Relating to the Freedom of Association and Protection
of the Right to Organise Convention, 1948 (No. 87) and the Right
to Organise and Collective Bargaining Convention, 1949 (No. 98).*
International Labour Conference, 58th Session, Geneva, 1973,
Report III (Part 4B), vi, 94 pp.

Freedom of Association: An International Survey. 1975, vii, 59 pp.

Trade Union Rights and Their Relation to Civil Liberties. International
Labour Conference, 54th Session, Geneva, 1970, Report VII, 70 pp.

Eligibility for Trade Union Office, 1972, ii, 86 pp. (D.27/1972).

Public Authorities and the Right to Protection of Trade Union Funds and Property. 1974, iii, 129 pp.

Bartolomei de la Cruz, H.G. *Protection Against Anti-Union Discrimination*, 1976, vii, 123 pp.

Caire, G. *Freedom of Association and Economic Development*, 1977, x, 159 pp.

Erstling, J.E. *The Right to Organise: A Survey of Laws and Regulations Relating to the Right of Workers to Establish Unions of Their Own Choosing*. 1977, 82 pp.

Gernigon, B. *Tenure of Trade Union Office*, 1977, vii, 112 pp.

Freedom of Association: Digest of Decisions of the Freedom of Association Committee of the Governing Body of the ILO. 2nd edition revised, 1976, xii, 180 pp.

Structure and Functions of Rural Workers' Organisations: A Workers' Education Manual. 1978, ix, 159 pp.

Trade Unions and the ILO: A Workers' Education Manual. 1979, viii, 96 pp.

Outline of the Existing Procedure for the Examination of Complaints Alleging Infringements of Trade Union Rights. 1977, 9 pp. (GB/LS/ March 1977).

von Potobsky, G. 'Protection of Trade Union Rights: Twenty Years' Work by the Committee on Freedom of Association.' *International Labour Review*, January 1972, pp. 69-83.

Reports of the Governing Body Committee on Freedom of Association, 1st-189th Reports, 1952-78

Report of the Fact-finding and Conciliation Commission on Freedom of Association concerning Persons Employed in the Public Sector in Japan, *Official Bulletin*, Vol. XLIX, No. 1, January 1966, Special Supplement, 536 pp.

Report of the Fact-finding and Conciliation Commission on Freedom of Association Concerning the Trade Union Situation in Greece, *Official Bulletin*, Vol. XLIX, No. 3, July 1966, special supplement, 87 pp.

Report of the Study Group to Examine the Labour and Trade Union Situation in Spain, *Official Bulletin*, Vol. LII, 1969, No. 4, second special supplement, viii, 298 pp.

Report of the Commission appointed under article 26 of the Constitution of the International Labour Organisation to examine the complaints concerning the observance by Greece of the Freedom of Association and Protection of the Right to Organise Convention,

1948 (No. 87), and the Right to Organise and Collective Bargaining
Convention, 1949 (No. 98), made by a number of delegates to the
52nd Session of the International Labour Conference, *Official
Bulletin*, Vol. LIV, 1971, No. 2, special supplement, 94 pp.

*The Trade Union Situation in Chile, Report of the Fact-Finding and
Conciliation Commission on Freedom of Association*. 1975, iv,
122 pp., annexes.

*Report of the Fact-Finding and Conciliation Commission on Freedom
of Association Concerning Lesotho*. 1975, 34 pp. (GB. 197/3/5).

*Discrimination (Employment and Occupation): General Conclusions on
the Reports Relating to the Convention (No. 111) and Recommendation (No. 111) Concerning Discrimination in Respect of Employment and Occupation, 1958*. International Labour Conference, 47th
Session, Geneva, 1963, Offprint from Report III (Part 4), pp. 171-262.

*Discrimination in Employment and Occupation: Standards and Policy
Statements Adopted Under the Auspices of the ILO*. 1967, 56 pp.

*Equality in Respect of Employment Under Legislation and Other
National Standards*, 1967, vi, 135 pp.

Equality of Opportunity in Employment in Asia: Problems and Policies.
Report and documents of a regional seminar, Manila, 2-11 December,
1969, 1970, 142 pp.

*Equality of Opportunity in Employment in the American Region:
Problems and Policies*. Report and documents of a regional symposium,
Panama, 1-12 October, 1973, 1974, 133pp.

*Equality of Opportunity and Treatment in Employment in the European
Region: Problems and Policies*. Report and documents of a regional
symposium, Geneva, 21-29 April 1975, iv, 89 pp.

*Equality of Opportunity and Treatment in Employment in Africa:
Problems and Policies*. Report of a regional symposium, Dakar, 19-29
September 1977, 15 pp.

*General Survey on the Reports Relating to the Discrimination (Employ-
ment and Occupation) Convention and Recommendation, 1958*.
International Labour Conference, 56th Session, Geneva, 1971, Report
III (Part 4B), 62 pp.

*Special National Procedures Concerning Non-Discrimination in Employ-
ment (With Particular Reference to the Private Sector) – A Practical
Guide*. 1975, 65 pp.

*Fighting Discrimination in Employment and Occupation: A Workers'
Education Manual*. Second impr., 1975, vii, 208 pp.

*Procedure for the Examination of Requests for 'Special Surveys' on
Situations Connected with the Elimination of Discrimination in*

Employment. 1974, 2 pp.

Report of the Commission Appointed Under Article 26 of the Constitution of the International Labour Organisation to Examine the Observance by Chile of the Hours of Work (Industry) Convention, 1919 (No. 1), and the Discrimination (Employment and Occupation) Convention, 1958 (No. 111), 1975, ii, 54 pp.

Report of the Committee Set Up to Consider the Representation Presented by the International Confederation of Free Trade Unions Under Article 24 of the Constitution Alleging Non-observance of the Discrimination (Employment and Occupation) Convention, 1958 (No. 111), by Czechoslovakia, Official Bulletin, Vol. LXI, 1978, Series A, No. 3 supplement, 61 pp.

INDEX

For Product Safety Concerns and Information please contact our EU
representative GPSR@taylorandfrancis.com
Taylor & Francis Verlag GmbH, Kaufingerstraße 24, 80331 München, Germany